Women, Work, and National Policy
The Kennedy–Johnson Years

Studies in
American History and Culture, No. 33

Robert Berkhofer, Series Editor

Director of American Culture Programs
and Richard Hudson Research Professor of History
The University of Michigan

Other Titles in This Series

Women, Work, and National Policy

The Kennedy–Johnson Years

by
Patricia G. Zelman

UMI RESEARCH PRESS
Ann Arbor, Michigan

305.4
Z 51

Produced and distributed by
UMI Research Press
an imprint of
University Microfilms International
Ann Arbor, Michigan 48106

Library of Congress Cataloging in Publication Data

Zelman, Patricia G.
   Women, work, and national policy.

   (Studies in American history and culture ; no. 33)
   Revision of thesis (Ph.D.)–Ohio State University, 1980.
   Bibliography: p.
   Includes index.
   1. Women–Government policy–United States–History.
I. Title. II. Series.

HQ1420.Z44 1982   305.4'0973   81-16351
ISBN 0-8357-1282-6   AACR2

For all my family

Contents

Acknowledgments

I happily acknowledge my debt to Robert H. Bremner, Professor of History at The Ohio State University. His gentle guidance helped me develop an appreciation for the historian's craft, and his devotion to scholarship has provided an inspiring model. I researched and wrote this study while living in Texas, and its completion would not have been possible without Professor Bremner's willingness to provide special long-distance assistance. I deeply appreciate his efforts, his patience, and his friendship.

Cynthia Harrison has generously shared the fruits of her research at the John F. Kennedy Library with me. I am indebted to her not only for that research, but for much of the conceptual framework of this essay, particularly regarding the Kennedy years. Her careful scholarship, her facility for finding order in a mass of seemingly chaotic events, and her willingness to share these talents with me have contributed heavily to whatever merits my essay possesses. Leila Rupp's incisive comments on the first four chapters of my draft have also been of benefit.

Material for the Johnson years comes primarily from the Lyndon Baines Johnson Library, Austin, Texas. Since the White House Central Files has no specific designation for "women," my topic necessitated much searching for materials, a task which was greatly facilitated by the Library's cooperative staff. I give special thanks to Nancy Smith, Claudia Anderson, and Tina Lawson for their cheerful and productive efforts. I am grateful to Judith A. Crosby for sharing with me her essay prospectus, "Executive Leadership in Policy-Issue Development: Women's Rights, A Case Study," which gave me important early leads. I also thank the staff at the National Archives Building, whose speedy retrieval of documents enhanced the productivity of my brief visit.

Esther Peterson, Martha Griffiths, Liz Carpenter, India Edwards, and Isabelle Shelton generously shared their time and insights with me. My friends in the Texas Women's Political Caucus used the "good ole girl network" to help me secure interviews; my thanks to Helen Martin, Ann Richards, and the Honorable Ernestine Glossbrenner.

I also wish to thank the staff of the Dick Smith Library at Tarleton State University, Stephenville, Texas. Harvey Gover's mastery of the Interlibrary Loan system has amazed and delighted me throughout the course of my research.

Donald Zelman has provided financial, moral, and many other kinds of support. He has shared, with patience and unfailing good humor, his considerable skills as historian, cook, housecleaner, and typist. I cheerfully acknowledge his contribution to this essay. I extend special thanks to Julie Grace Zelman for believing I could do it.

List of Abbreviations

bfoq	Bona fide occupational qualification
CAC	Citizens' Advisory Council on the Status of Women
EEOC	Equal Employment Opportunity Commission
ERA	Equal Rights Amendment
FEPC	Fair Employment Practices Commission
ICSW	Interdepartmental Committee on the Status of Women
LBJL	Lyndon Baines Johnson Library, Austin, Texas
NA	National Archives Building, Washington, D.C.
NWP	National Woman's Party
PCEEO	President's Committee on Equal Employment Opportunity
PCSW	President's Commission on the Status of Women
RDOL	Records of the Department of Labor, 1963–1969, Lyndon Baines Johnson Library
WB	Women's Bureau, Department of Labor
WWW	Records of the Secretary of Labor, W. Willard Wirtz

Introduction

Legal enunciations of equal employment opportunity for women as a policy of the U.S. government occurred within the relatively brief period from 1963 to 1967, but the development of this policy was linked to several longer-term occurrences. One of these was the civil rights movement, which formulated the concept of equal employment opportunity as the keystone of a strategy for upgrading black economic status. During the high pitch of civil rights activism in the mid-1960s, this concept was extended to include women. It thereby connected with a second long-term process, the debate about women's proper role—in society generally, and in the workplace in particular. Women's inclusion in the remedies developed to correct racial employment discrimination gave new focus to an old and stale debate between proponents of an Equal Rights Amendment and advocates of protective labor legislation. During the start of this new phase of the debate over women's role, actions taken by the federal government helped define the political and legal concerns that sparked the modern feminist movement and dominated its early stages.

The origins of the modern feminist movement are diffuse, and the forces underlying its development occurred over a long period. The movement has no precise starting point, but the formation of the National Organization for Women (NOW) in 1966 marks a critical juncture in its development; NOW was the first nationally oriented, avowedly feminist group organized since the 1920s. In the years immediately following 1966, support for feminist ideas grew and feminist organizations multiplied. According to Jo Freeman, chronicler of the various modern feminist groups, the movement had reached a "take-off point" by 1970.[1]

By that time, equal employment opportunity for women had been enunciated as national policy and its legal bases established by two acts of Congress and an Executive Order. The Equal Pay Act of 1963 required employers covered by the federal Fair Labor Standards Act to pay equal wages for equal work, regardless of the employees' sex. Title VII of the Civil Rights Act of 1964 forbade certain private employers from discriminating on the basis of sex (along with race, color, religion or national origin) in any personnel actions. Executive Order 11375 extended the ban on sex discrimination in hiring to the federal government and to contractors receiving government funds, requiring them to take "affirmative action" to insure equal employment opportunity. The Executive Order was promulgated in October, 1967, one year after NOW's organization, and before the movement attracted much attention.

The early political efforts of the women's movement focused on attaining enforcement of these already enacted laws. This situation is an anomalous one for a reform group, and forms an especially marked contrast to the method by which legal mandates of equal employment opportunity for blacks were attained. If one envisions a "normal" sequence of events for a successful political reform, it would begin with a definition of the perceived problem, and lead eventually to the offering of a proposed legislative solution by the interested group. Public debate would follow, as the proponents of reform try to educate and win support from the public, and as opposition to the reform is expressed and organized. Legislative action would next be attempted, compromises weighed and made, and a law designed to be as unobjectionable to as many people as possible would emerge as a sign of the legislative body's interpretation of the public's consensus.

The enactment of laws mandating equal employment opportunity for blacks generally followed the above outline, although the process was lengthy, beginning at least as early as the 1941 proposal for a march on Washington. The legislative remedy eventually proposed for the problem of racial discrimination in employment called for government involvement in the personnel policies of private businesses. Before the public would accept this drastic and politically sensitive measure, compelling need had to be shown. Eventual public acceptance resulted from the efforts of a massive "people's movement" to which thousands of persons, hoping to further the cause of racial justice, sacrificed time, energy, social position, economic security, and in some cases, their lives.[2]

When Title VII of the Civil Rights Act of 1964 outlawed racial discrimination at the hiring gate, and Executive Order 11246 required governmental contractors to establish "affirmative action" programs to recruit minority group employees, the public had a fairly clear sense of what these laws meant and why they were being enacted: the proponents of reform had won. Enforcing the laws was another matter, requiring further efforts of a different sort, but these efforts were facilitated to some extent by the public debate that preceded the legislation.

Equal employment opportunity for women, however, became a national policy with relatively little public debate. There was no "people's movement" to arouse public awareness, no powerful pressure group to push for such policy, no national debate on the issue's merits, as had been the case with the racial question. These all came later, partly as a result of the previous establishment of the legal bases for the policy.

Commentators have thus observed that the women's movement achieved its earliest political victories by riding the coattails of the civil rights movement. There is much truth in the observation; certainly Title VII of the Civil Rights Act of 1964 and Executive Order 11375 were direct outgrowths of the movement for racial equality, and the organizations that sprang up in the late 1960s and early 1970s to defend women's legal rights were consciously patterned after similar black lobbying and pressure groups. The coattail view does not, however, account for the Equal Pay Act, which was achieved through more traditional political methods before the spurt of civil rights legislation in the mid-1960s. Nor does it adequately explain the process by which the issue of gender became attached to the racial issue's coattails. As the coattail view implies, political events helped goad the movement into existence and determined the way it took shape. But not all these events are related to the civil rights movement. The political origins of modern feminism have a history of their own. This essay examines a part of that history, and attempts to augment the coattail view by focusing on the development of a federal policy of equal employment opportunity for women during the years just prior to feminism's "take off."

Because social attitudes towards women's place failed to coincide with the objective circumstances of women's lives, conditions had been "ripe" for a feminist movement for some years before one developed; looking back, one senses a certain inevitability about it. But even inevitable events, if there are such things, must have some means of becoming actualized. This essay emphasizes political sources of the women's movement, but the author has no wish to suggest that these sources are a primary or even necessary cause of its being. Demographic, economic, cultural and psychosocial factors all played crucial roles, and politics, even in a democracy, reflects these developments imperfectly at best. A satisfactory explanation of feminism's rebirth requires an analysis of how these, and possibly other, factors interacted.

Such an analysis also needs to account for the development of grass roots feminist groups which arose within leftist groups and from other sources shortly after NOW was organized.[3] Composed primarily of college-aged women who were active in the civil rights and antiwar movements, and who harbored antiestablishment views, these grass roots feminist groups were more interested in developing new ways to effect social and cultural change than in working through traditional political channels. Although the relationship between these groups and the generally older, women's rights-oriented people who supported NOW has yet to be fully delineated, both segments of the movement were crucial to feminism's rebirth and its sustained growth, if for no other reason than the diversity they gave to feminist appeals, tactics, goals, and thought. The grass roots feminist groups have been omitted from this study not because the author thinks them insig-nificant, but simply because they were, by their own choice, not working in the traditional political context with which this study deals.

Chapter 1 traces the development of the argument between equality and protection which began in the 1920s, and provides a background for under-standing women's political situation in 1960 when John Kennedy took office and Esther Peterson became Director of the Women's Bureau in the Department of Labor and, more importantly, Kennedy's informal deputy for women's affairs. Under Peterson's direction, executive attention to women's political affairs veered away from the emphasis of previous administrations on token appointments of women to high office and focused instead on stimulating public discussion of women's status and building support for legislative proposals to benefit women workers. Chapter 2 examines the policy initiatives of the Kennedy years, including passage of the Equal Pay Act, and creation of a President's Commission on the Status of Women. The PCSW exerted a stronger influence than one might expect from a governmental commission, for in addition to initiating discussion of women's changing status and setting an agenda of modest reforms, it inspired the creation of similar commissions in most of the states, thus creating a network of persons concerned with advancing women's interests through political channels.

The fruits of Peterson's approach were not immediately apparent, however, and women party leaders, whose advice Kennedy ignored, decried his poor record on female appointments. Their criticism gave Lyndon Johnson an issue on which he could out-perform Kennedy; acceding to the Presidency barely a year before the next election, Johnson desperately needed such issues. Chapter 3 discusses Johnson's efforts to woo women's support by a spate of highly publicized female appointments and a series of speeches lamenting women's "underutilization" in the American economy. Johnson's rhetorical support dwindled as he became engrossed in the War on Poverty, but his presidential blessing for the cause of women's advance-ment provided an important source of strength for the PCSW's bureaucratic successors, the Interdepartmental Commission, and the Citizens' Advisory Committee on the Status of Women.

Early in 1964, as President Johnson tried to enhance his political fortunes by raising the issue of women's employment, Southern Congress-men used the same issue to ridicule and weaken the administration's omnibus Civil Rights Bill. Chapter 4 focuses on the strange set of circumstances that led to Congressional approval of an amendment to Title VII of that bill, adding sex to race and the other bases upon which employment discrimination was prohibited. Because this sudden and unexpected linkage of race and sex discrimination threatened to invalidate women's protective laws, the old debate between equality and protection resurfaced in new and more vital form.

During the period between the sex amendment's passage and Title VII's effective date, the federal Status of Women groups tried to develop policy recommendations for the agency established to enforce the law, the Equal Employment Opportunity Commission (EEOC). Conflicting attitudes regarding the benefits and desirability of protective legislation stymied their efforts. During this same period, however, a feminist viewpoint began to crystallize within the Status of Women groups. Chapter 5 shows how this new attitude developed from perceptions of an antiwoman bias in the administration's War on Poverty, evidenced by lack of support for the Women's Job Corps and the revealing phrases of the Moynihan Report. Chapter 6 explains how the failure of the new EEOC to enforce Title VII's sex provisions with the same energy it devoted to ending racial discrimination contributed to the further development of a feminist consciousness among the Status of Women groups and their allies. Increasingly, the defenders of women's interests began to accept the premise that the issue of sexual equality was neither separate from nor less important than racial equality, but part of the broader issue of human rights. Such an outlook was inimical to the protectionist philosophy.

The concluding chapter of this study delineates the process by which the legal linkage of sex and race discrimination was completed with President Johnson's promulgation of Executive Order 11375. It also explores some of the implications of that linkage, and, in conclusion, reviews the essay to find evidence of the increasing democratization of the process for formulating women's policy.

1

Equality vs. Protection, 1920–1960

The demand for equal employment opportunity for women is at least as old as the women's rights movement. The "Declaration of Sentiments" adopted at the first women's rights convention in 1848 at Seneca Falls, New York, included lack of such opportunity in its list of grievances that women suffered under the tyranny of men:

> He has monopolized nearly all the profitable employments, and from those she is permitted to follow, she receives but a scanty remuneration. He closes against her all the avenues to wealth and distinction which he considers most honorable to himself.

The convention also adopted a resolution directed at this problem:

> *Resolved*, That the speedy success of our cause depends upon the zealous and untiring efforts of both men and women for the securing to woman an equal participation with men in the various trades, professions, and commerce.[1]

The employment issue, along with many others raised by the early feminists, was set aside around the turn of the century as the movement for women's rights came to focus almost exclusively on the attainment of suffrage. Shortly after the Nineteenth Amendment was ratified in 1920, laws affecting women's employment became a source of dispute between two factions of the former suffrage movement.

Although few people took part in—or even noticed—this conflict, it dominated the discussion of governmental policy regarding women for the next four decades. This chapter will examine the origins and development of this long-term debate which pitted an abstract ideal of legal equality against the limited but pragmatic benefits of special protections for women workers. It will then offer some explanations for the government's failure to develop a policy regarding working women despite the dramatic increase of women in the labor force between 1920 and 1960. This information provides a background for understanding the relatively rapid development of a national policy of equal employment for women during the 1960s.

During the suffrage campaign, members of the militant Congressional Union generated considerable publicity by chaining themselves to the White House fence, fasting and undergoing force-feeding in Washington jails. Once the vote for women was secure, these energetic and dedicated women reorganized as the National Woman's Party (NWP) and embarked on a new crusade to eliminate all remaining laws discriminating against women. Among those laws, according to the NWP, were various state statutes regulating conditions of employment for women but not for men. The NWP's campaign brought it into direct conflict with the Women's Bureau in the Department of Labor and a loose coalition of reformers whose goal was to extend and augment protective labor legislation for women.

Women's protective laws were an outgrowth of earlier unsuccessful attempts by Progessive reformers to establish laws protecting all workers from various abuses, particularly from long hours and low wages.[2] The U.S. Supreme Court had consistently invalidated such laws on the grounds that they infringed upon individual freedom of contract. Eventually, reformers were able to win Supreme Court approval for laws affecting only women workers by arguing that women were a special class because of their child-bearing capacity. The protection of women's health, the argument went, was of such importance to the well-being of the race that it overrode considerations of contractual freedom. In 1908 the Court accepted this position in the case of *Muller* v. *Oregon*, upholding an Oregon law stipulating maximum working hours for women. Reform groups then began a long and arduous campaign to get women's protective legislation passed and strengthened in the states.

When the U.S. entered World War I and unprecedented numbers of women were drawn into the labor force, reformers, particularly those involved in the women's trade union movement, feared that protective laws would be ignored in the rush for war production. An investigative commission, a typically Progressive device, was established at first in the Ordnance Department to oversee conditions and hours of women working in munitions plants. In 1918 a commission with broader concerns, Women in Industry Service, began operations in the Department of Labor. It was given permanent statutory status as the Women's Bureau of the Department of Labor in 1920. The enabling legislation charged the Bureau to:

> formulate standards and policies which shall promote the welfare of wage-earning women, improve their working conditions, increase their efficiency, and advance their opportunities for profitable employment. This said Bureau shall have authority to investigate and report to said department on all matters pertaining to the welfare of women in industry.[3]

The Bureau's first director was Mary Anderson, a shoemaker who had risen through the ranks of the Women's Trade Union League, and was staunchly devoted to the women's labor movement. Holding the directorship from 1920 until 1944, she firmly established a labor-oriented, protectionist stance for the Bureau, and developed its clientele from trade unions and like-minded reform groups. Trade union women, with a few exceptions, had not been particularly interested in securing woman's suffrage or equal legal rights as defined by the NWP. Their concerns were of a more immediate and practical nature: melioration of sweatshop conditions, limitation of daily and weekly working hours, job security, a minimum wage to cover living costs for the worker and any dependents, and pay commensurate with that received by men doing similar work.[4]

Elements of the suffrage movement, particularly those former members of the National American Woman Suffrage Association who formed the League of Women Voters in 1920, shared the viewpoint of the trade union women regarding protective legislation and allied with the WB and the Women's Trade Union League to help press for its enactment. Other groups participating at various times in this loose coalition included the National Consumers' League, the Young Women's Christian Association, National Council of Catholic Women, National Council of Jewish Women, and the Women's Christian Temperance Union.

Viewing themselves as humanitarian social reformers fighting for the rights of an oppressed working class, the supporters of protective legislation encountered tremendous opposition from business and industrial interests. Such opposition was expected, and made sense in terms of the reformers' view of the economic and political system. Opposition from the NWP was not so easily understood, and, therefore, all the more vexing. Recognizing the real benefits that protective legislation afforded working women, the reformers felt that NWP was betraying women's true interests. They resented having to spend their limited energies rebutting NWP arguments which, they felt, were hopelessly idealistic and insensitive to the needs of lower-class women.

The NWP did not object to protective laws as such, but to any laws applying only to women. While the reformers of the WB coalition sought to advance women's status by a variety of broad social reforms, only part of which related strictly to women's concerns, the feminists of the NWP had only one goal: absolute legal equality of the sexes. Exhibiting a naive conception of law's function, the NWP held that legal distinctions were the basis of women's inferior status; women could advance neither socially nor economically until these distinctions were removed. Measures designed to give women special treatment in the labor market were impediments to equality, for they perpetuated the idea that women were a special class in need of protection. This was exactly what the reformers had been arguing, and the NWP believed the argument was shortsighted, pernicious, and contrary to the best interests of all women, regardless of economic class.

In 1923 at a conference commemorating the seventy-fifth anniversary of the Seneca Falls Convention, the NWP proposed a Constitutional amendment designed to remove women's second-class legal status. The Equal Rights Amendment (ERA), whose enactment became the NWP's sole concern for the next half century, held that, "Men and women shall have equal rights throughout the United States and every place subject to its jurisdiction."[5] Securing sponsors for the amendment, and lobbying vigorously in its behalf, the NWP managed to have it introduced into the 68th Congress in 1923 and in every subsequent session until its eventual passage in 1972.[6]

Unlike the Nineteenth Amendment, which was clear and specific in its intent, the proposed Equal Rights Amendment was phrased in broad and vaguely defined terms. The task of giving practical definitions to "equal rights" would fall ultimately upon the Supreme Court, a prospect that horrified the WB and other proponents of protective legislation. In 1923, the same year the ERA was introduced, the Court's ruling in *Adkins* v. *Children's Hospital* sent reformers into deep despair. The Adkins decision not only nullified a District of Columbia minimum wage law for women, but threatened other protective legislation as well, for the majority opinion held that the premises on which the Muller decision of 1908 had been based no longer obtained; women, having the vote, now had an equality with men that obviated the need for special legislation.[7] The NWP filed a brief with the Court requesting such a ruling.[8]

As historian William O'Neill notes, the reformers were too demoralized by the Court's attacks on labor legislation to "respond fairly to proposals that even marginally complicated their position," as the ERA certainly did.[9] Legal advice sought by the WB confirmed fears that the Amendment would invalidate state protective laws.[10] The vague wording of the amendment, coupled with the unsympathetic tenor of the Supreme Court aroused other fears as well. No one could predict the possible effects of the ERA on laws governing such diverse matters as inheritance, property ownership, support for wives and children, divorce, mothers' pensions, and rape. The ERA, warned one legal expert, "would operate like a blind man with a shot gun."[11] The Women's Bureau, the Women's Trade Union League, the League of Women Voters, and the National Consumers' League, along with other reform-minded groups, thus joined in opposing the amendment.

The positions of the WB and NWP reflect a deep philosophical split over the question of woman's role in society. In arguing that there were both good and bad discriminations against women, the WB showed its pragmatic acceptance of society's belief that women were different from men. Through its studies, the Bureau had challenged the generally held notion that woman's place was solely in the home. It argued, and collected statistics to prove, that many women did work, and did so chiefly for reasons of economic need, often under conditions of great hardship. But it accepted society's axiom that women bore primary responsibility for the home, and argued that because housework and child care lay heavy burdens on working women, they needed special protections in the marketplace. Thus the WB and the reformers with whom it cooperated sought to ease working women's load by lessening the pressures of their jobs and their potential for exploitation in the marketplace. They accurately saw themselves as political realists, working to improve conditions for women in ways that were feasible, if difficult. Their experiences, as well as the statistics they collected, told them that women were different from men, and they believed it the height of folly to treat the sexes identically. The ERA, they argued, would force women to shoulder unequal burdens. Only through special protections could women hope to achieve any sort of equality with men.

The NWP was interested not in making women's status more tolerable but in changing it. Focusing on the abstract principle of equality rather than on the practical effects of policies, NWP members defined equality in a Jeffersonian sense, synonymous with liberty or freedom from artificial restraints. They believed that women, given equal opportunity with men, could take care of themselves. The realities of the status quo were, to them, simply proof that women had been treated unfairly. The situation would not be altered by patchwork legislation; relief for women would come only through recognition of the fundamental equality of the sexes.

This ideological stance assumed that women's place was wherever she chose it to be. But by focusing only on legal restrictions to women's choices, the NWP placed enormous faith in the ability and desire of individual women to overcome the social and cultural limits to choice implied in the concept of "women's place." Because it failed to address such questions as who, if not women, would be responsible for the home, NWP's narrow legalism in effect forced upon women a choice men did not have to make: the choice between career and family. The overwhelming majority of women opted, consciously or not, for families and remained uninterested in furthering their status as women.

Lack of public enthusiasm for women's equality did not deter the NWP, for its strategy did not depend on mass support. NWP founder Alice Paul, who learned militant feminist tactics from the Pankhursts in England, believed that a few strategically placed and knowledgeable women could achieve their goal by lobbying and harassing government officials. This strategy was better suited to England, with its system of strong party loyalty, than to the U.S., where political power was more widely diffused, but Paul and her followers believed it had been decisive in securing the Nineteenth Amendment. Downplaying the role of the National American Woman Suffrage Association in building broad-based, state-by-state support for women's suffrage, Paul and her followers felt such organization was unnecessary. Their strategy had been vindicated once; there was no need to revise it. Their stand on equal rights for women was just; members had only to defend it energetically and persistently, and everything else would eventually fall into place.

The NWP thus concentrated its efforts on Congressional lobbying and securing endorsement from important political figures. The organization maintained a permanent and well-organized lobbying force in Washington. NWP lobbyists argued convincingly at Congressional hearings, but their most successful tactic appears to have been sheer persistence. Members of the WB coalition charged that legislators agreed to support the amendment simply to avoid further harassment from NWP lobbyists.[12]

Endorsing the ERA was a safe action for a legislator; few people outside of Congress had even heard of it, so there was little chance of voter reprisal. Nor was there much chance that the Amendment would come to a vote. The idea of equal rights, moreover, was attractive in the abstract; the phrase had a democratic ring, and it was difficult to argue that any citizen should not have equal rights under the law.

WB Director Mary Anderson paid tribute to the ERA's appeal by condemning it as "nothing more than a good slogan."[13] She and other ERA opponents felt the NWP was politically naive, but nevertheless viewed its efforts with alarm. Historian William Chafe, studying the records of the League of Women Voters and Women's Trade Union League, concluded that these groups seem to have devoted "an inordinate amount of time and energy" to working against the amendment.[14]

Dissension among protectionists and ERA supporters remained a hurdle to further political activity on behalf of women throughout the 1930s and 1940s, but neither group was willing to compromise. In 1936, working with leaders of several women's groups, particularly the Women's Trade Union League, Mary Anderson helped draw up a positive program designed to effect a compromise on the issues of equal rights and protective legislation. The framers hoped that all major women's groups would endorse the statement of principles contained in the Woman's Charter, and use their agreement as a base from which to work for legislation to improve women's status. Their efforts were in vain. The NWP objected to the Charter, and more sympathetic organizations were unable to adjust their programs to accommodate joint action. Anderson termed the effort "a complete flop."[15]

Protectionists suffered another setback in 1937 when the National Federation of Business and Professional Women's Clubs (BPW) declared its support for the ERA and joined the NWP lobbying effort. The BPW was a prestigious group with a larger membership and greater respectability than the NWP. Its members were chiefly white-collar women workers; they apparently feared the possibility that protective legislation would be extended to executive and professional positions, precluding women from holding high paying executive jobs which required occasional long hours of work.

An opportunity for the old dispute to be settled arose in 1938 with passage of the federal Fair Labor Standards Act, which, along with a change in the Supreme Court's mood, made protective labor standards for men a reality. But because many state laws set higher standards for women than the bare minima required by the FLSA, protectionists continued their support for laws applying only to women.

In the 1940s, the WB coalition made another attempt to silence ERA proponents. It lobbied for the creation of a Congressional commission to investigate women's status, presuming that it would conclude that women were better off without the ERA. But the Woman's Status bill, twice introduced by Representative Emmanuel Celler (D., N.Y.), did not pass.[16]

Despite its preoccupation with the ERA, the WB did undertake other activities. It argued persistently, and with some success, for example, against Depression-inspired legislation that would have limited the jobs available to married women with employed spouses. Such restrictions were contrary to American practice, Bureau officials contended, because they followed the Marxian tenet of awarding jobs on the basis of need rather than ability.[17]

On a more positive note, the Bureau sought to arouse interest in state and federal legislation guaranteeing that women performing the same work as men would receive equal pay. It managed to secure clauses requiring equal pay in some of the regulatory orders issued by the War Labor Boards during both World Wars, and in various NRA codes during the New Deal.[18] The first federal legislation relating specifically to equal pay was introduced in 1945, in acknowledgment of women's contribution to the war effort. The "Women's Equal Pay Bill" did not pass, nor did any of the 104 similar bills introduced from the 79th to the 87th Congresses.[19] Opposition from the business community and a general feeling that the problem was neither widespread nor urgent are the apparent reasons for this failure.

In 1952 the WB brought together representatives of women's organizations, trade unions, employer associations, and civic groups to organize the National Committee for Equal Pay which began to lobby for a bill.[20] The NWP refused to join the lobby effort, contending that the ERA would take care of equal pay along with a host of other legal ills suffered by women. The National Committee for Equal Pay aroused some interest in the issue, and helped get bills introduced into Congress, but no hearings were held on the matter from 1950 until 1962.

Equal pay fared somewhat better in state legislatures. The first state equal pay legislation came in Michigan and Montana in 1919, but no further states passed such laws until World War II, when four more states did so. Between 1946 and 1953, nine more states joined the list.[21] WB leaders regarded these laws as victories, but most were vaguely worded and lacked enforcement provisions.[22]

The strain of opposing the Equal Rights Amendment continued to plague the WB, contributing to its ineffectiveness in other areas. During the 1940s, the General Federation of Women's Clubs joined the NWP and BPW's lobby effort, and proponents managed to secure endorsement of the ERA in both the Democratic and Republican party platforms. ERA supporters also secured expressions of approval from Presidents Truman and Eisenhower. In 1950, and again in 1953, the ERA passed the Senate, but both times a rider exempting protective legislation made the bill unacceptable to its proponents.[23]

In 1960 the situation remained at an impasse. Protectionists were unable to finesse this persistent issue, but the ERA stood little chance of passage; even had it met Congressional approval, it is unlikely that a sufficient number of states would have approved its ratification. The WB continued to support special legislative protections for women workers and to object to the ERA in general terms as well. Neither the terms of the debate nor the limited context in which it was conducted had changed substantially since the 1920s; the argument between abstract equality and specific protections continued to be made by small groups of women in Washington talking mainly to themselves.

As the debate dragged on, women were moving into the work force in unprecedented numbers, causing women, families, and the work force itself to undergo tremendous changes. Women's employment increased sharply during World War II, and while both numbers and percentages of women employees dropped after the war, they did not return to their prewar levels. (See Table 1.) Following the postwar adjustment, the female labor force increased at a rate much greater than that of males, so that the female proportion of all workers rose from one-fourth in 1940 to one-third in 1960.[24] The female labor force nearly doubled between 1940 and 1960, with married women and mothers forming a large portion of the new entrants. The bulk of the female labor force had traditionally been composed of single women; by 1960 married women accounted for more than half of all working women. (See Table 2.)

The implications of these changes were significant enough to justify intense governmental interest, but apart from the old ERA debate—which few politicians took seriously—and the drive for an equal pay bill— spearheaded by the largely ineffective WB—there was little evidence of concern. Division among the ranks of politically active women over the

Table 1. Women in the Labor Force by Marital Status 1940–1960[a]

Marital Status	Employed Women						
	1940	1944	1948	1952	1955	1958	1960

Number (Millions)

Marital Status	1940	1944	1948	1952	1955	1958	1960
Single	6.7	7.5	5.9	5.5	5.1	5.4	5.4
Married, husband present	4.2	6.2	7.6	9.2	10.4	11.8	12.3
No children under 18	2.7	b	4.4	5.0	5.2	5.7	5.7
Children 6–17 only	1.5	b	1.9	2.5	3.2	3.7	4.1
Children 0–5			1.2	1.7	2.0	2.4	2.5
Widowed, divorced, living apart	2.9	4.7	3.7	4.1	4.6	4.8	4.9
All women	13.9	18.5	17.2	18.8	20.1	22.0	22.6

Percent

Marital Status	1940	1944	1948	1952	1955	1958	1960
Single	48.1	58.6	51.1	50.0	46.6	45.4	44.1
Married, husband present	14.7	21.7	22.0	25.3	27.7	30.2	30.5
No children under 18		b	28.4	30.9	32.7	38.8	34.7
Children 6–17 only	8.6	b	26.0	31.1	34.7	37.6	39.0
Children 0–5			10.7	13.9	16.0	18.2	18.6
Widowed, divorced, living apart	35.4	42.0	38.3	38.8	38.5	40.8	40.0
All women	25.7	35.0	31.0	32.7	33.4	35.0	34.8

a. From Ivan F. Nye and Lois W. Hoffman, "The Socio-Cultural Setting," in *The Other Half: Roads to Women's Equality*, ed. by Cynthia F. Epstein and William J. Goode (Englewood Cliffs, New Jersey, 1971), p. 88.
b. Information not available.

Table 2. Percent Distribution of Women In the Labor Force by Marital Status, 1940–1960[a]

Marital Status	Percent		
	1940	1950	1960
Single	49	32	24
Married, husband present	30	48	54
Widowed, divorced, or separated	21	20	22

a. From United States Women's Bureau, *1969 Handbook on Women Workers*, Bulletin 294 (Washington, D.C., 1969), p. 24. Data include employed women aged 14 and over in March of each year.

ERA in 1960, as throughout the preceding forty years, made it easier for the government to ignore questions relating to women, and the impotence of the Women's Bureau (the one governmental agency charged with formulating programs to aid women workers) further facilitated federal passivity.

Chartered in 1920 as an investigative and educational agency, the Bureau never moved beyond these functions. Its status was linked to the strength of its potential clients—groups of women whose interests it might serve, and from whom it could receive political support, much as the Department of Labor served unions and the Department of Agriculture served organized farmers. The withering of the Women's Trade Union League and the National Consumers' League in the 1930s diminished important sources of backing and support.[25] Failure of a "woman's vote" to materialize, coupled with the conservatism and lack of political interest on the part of remaining women's organizations left the Bureau with no political power base. Bureau leaders tried to form one by bringing together representatives of women's organizations to work for specific goals such as the Woman's Charter and the Equal Pay Bill, but met little success. Without a powerful clientele, the WB had only minimal input into policy decisions. Its main focus remained on developing public awareness of the facts of working women's situation. Even this limited role was difficult in a society determined to believe that women belonged at home. The Bureau could report that women were subject to discrimination and suggest possible remedies, but since so few people paid attention, it could not persuade the government to act.

The Bureau's political weakness was a manifestation of the general social indifference to the concerns of working women. At bottom, it was this lack of public interest that allowed the government to ignore working women. Matters relating specifically to women were simply not viewed as political issues by the overwhelming majority of Americans, including women themselves. There are several explanations, none entirely satisfactory, for this phenomenon.

An historical scenario may be constructed to show that the "time was not ripe," the historical climate unfavorable. During the 1920s women's failure to vote as a block, and the smear campaign linking feminism and bolshevism, discredited feminism and stymied its further ideological and political development.[26] The college-educated "new woman," who might have been expected to carry on the feminist fight, expressed the same aversion to politics as the rest of her generation and focused instead on personal liberation. Popularized Freudian psychology reinforced the old concept of "woman's sphere" with scientific terminology and implied that women's problems were personal, not societal or political.

Women suffered along with everyone else through the Great Depression, and although women, particularly as social workers, became more numerous in government service during the New Deal, the political questions with which they dealt centered on matters of general welfare rather than on the problems of women specifically. During World War II, "Rosie the Riveter" and her cohorts went to work in record numbers, but at war's end they were encouraged to move to the suburbs, help produce the baby boom, and become engrossed in the cult of family "togetherness."

All these generalizations are accurate enough; conditions during the period 1920–60 conspired against the development of women's political consciousness, and "feminist" became a disparaging term. But in view of the larger historical precedent, public apathy towards women's advancement needs no particular explanation: it is the norm. Even during the suffrage campaign, which might seem a propitious time for its development, feminism's appeal was limited.

Another variation on the theme of unfavorable historical climate deals with the feminists' failure to articulate an ideology and clearly define their goals. William O'Neill has developed this line of thought most fully, noting the difficulty feminists faced in developing a logically consistent philosophy.[27] By choosing to work for immediate rather than long-term goals, and adopting acceptable rather than radical rationales, nineteenth and early twentieth century feminists managed to make higher education and the vote for women respectable but failed to suggest what women should do with their education and their votes. They had, in effect, no clear idea of what it meant, or ought to mean, to be a woman in America. This failure, O'Neill contends, "permitted" feminism to "collapse once equal suffrage had been secured."[28]

The central importance of employment as a means to economic security, independence, and personal fulfillment had been recognized by early feminists, but their answer to the problem of improving women's employment status had been the renunciation of marriage, an idea which most women rejected. Feminist theorist Charlotte Perkins Gilman offered the practical suggestion that housework and child care be professionalized so that women could participate in the job market on equal terms with men, but her pioneering efforts went unheeded.[29] The difficulty lay not in developing an ideology as such, but in developing one that was acceptable as well as consistent. Again one encounters the unfavorable historical climate.

The sterile debate over the ERA had certain ideological trappings, but neither the NWP nor the WB coalition had a workable solution to the problem of women's inferior status. The NWP held out the abstract goal of equality but ignored the practical hurdles imposed by social conventions. The WB's position assumed the primacy of women's family responsibilities, but held out no inspiring visions for the career advancement of women, and no goals other than decent working conditions, a living wage, and equal pay for equal work. These goals were sufficiently radical in a political sense to make their attainment difficult, and assuredly their achievement would have benefitted working women. However, they had not been designed to serve as an ideology for the general advancement of women's status, and they did not do so.

Yet the very lack of clearly defined goals for working women, of a feminist ideology, and of any coherent governmental policy may well have contributed to the easy entry of large numbers of women into the labor force, a movement which accelerated rapidly after World War II despite all the encouragements (official and otherwise) for women to return home from their wartime jobs. Carl Degler has speculated that the movement of women into the work force was so easy and aroused so little opposition precisely because it was the result of thousands of individual, private decisions rather than part of a feminist crusade which would have threatened traditional values and smacked of the ideology which Americans have traditionally found so distasteful.[30]

The fact that women entered the labor force as the result of private choices had an important corollary: any problems women faced in combining the dual roles of worker and homemaker were private problems. The social implications of women's work—at home as well as in the market-place—were thus denied, and the possibility of dealing with problems on a collective basis was stymied.

Aside from the personal adjustments confronting working women and their families, women employees faced the more obviously collective problem of job discrimination. Women held jobs in every category listed by the census, but they were not evenly dispersed throughout the labor force. Very few were professionals or executives; most held low paying, dead-end "women's jobs." In 1960 about half of all employed women worked in occupations in which 75 percent or more of the total workers were female.[31] The low status of these jobs was reflected in women's wages; the median wage for fulltime, year-round women workers in 1960 was 61 percent of that for males.[32]

This sexual segregation of the labor force resulted from a complex set of circumstances, including women's "willingness" to accept low status, low paying jobs, and the rapid relative growth rates of certain occupational categories such as clerical work in which women had previously established a foothold.[33] But the attitudes held by working women and employers alike were a crucial element in the establishment and perpetuation of a sex-segregated labor market. Women, it was believed, were "secondary" workers, with no permanent attachment to the labor force. They were interested in jobs, not careers. Family responsibilities mitigated their devotion to their market work, and they were thus incapable of holding responsible positions. Women were, moreover, best suited to jobs like teaching, nursing, and secretarial work, which related to their traditional role of nurturer and helper.

The relationship between "women's jobs" and "women's place" was more linguistic than functional. Secretaries worked as supportive aides to male executives, just as women were supportive to their husbands, but few wives used a typewriter at home. Teachers nurtured children, but a woman responsible for forty children all the same age with widely divergent backgrounds was not performing the same services she would for her own children.[34] These contrived explanations suggest that the creation of a "place" for women in the labor market was a means of reconciling a conflict between long-held attitudes and recently-changed behavior.

"Ever since World War II," writes Chafe, "the reality of woman's 'place' had ceased to conform to the stereotype."[35] This attitudinal lag offers the most plausible explanation for the lack of political interest in working women's issues. Emotional investment in the idea of "women's place" was so intense that attitudes failed to respond to the overwhelming evidence of millions of working women. Looking at the situation politically would acknowledge its existence, would challenge both the old attitudes and the new behavior, and unleash strong emotional reactions. This is the kind of situation astute politicians avoid. So long as there was no demand for it to do so, the government would not try to deal with the problems of working women; these remained private matters.

It is, then, not surprising that Congress avoided serious consideration of the ERA, nor that the aging but still persistent lobbyists of the NWP became the butt of congressional jokes about "tennis shoe ladies."[36] Nor is it remarkable that Presidential attention to matters relating to women remained minimal.

Presidents Truman and Eisenhower endorsed the ERA, but neither was sufficiently foolhardy to push the issue. Eisenhower also expressed support for an equal pay bill.[37] Yet evidence of presidential concern for women voters was confined mainly to the appointment of a few women to high government positions. These appointments were not entirely noncontroversial—objections from male bureaucrats stalled at least several proposed appointments.[38] But they provided a relatively safe way for Presidents to acknowledge women without raising the painful issues involved in the attitudinal lag. As long as the numbers of female appointees remained small, women holding high government posts were rightly viewed as exceptional, and provided no threat to the status quo.

President Taft made the first appointment of a woman to a major government post by naming Julia Lathrop to head the Children's Bureau in

1912, even before women won the vote.[39] Each of Taft's successors included women among his appointees, but the greatest gains in female appointments came during Franklin Roosevelt's tenure. Prodded by his wife and by Molly Dewson, who ran the Women's Division of the Democratic National Committee, Roosevelt surpassed his predecessors both in the number of women he appointed and in the importance of the posts he selected for them. His appointment of the first woman Federal District Judge, Florence E. Allen, and of the first female Cabinet member, Secretary of Labor Frances Perkins, were especially gratifying to party women.

Both Truman and Eisenhower continued Roosevelt's practice: each relied on one trusted woman, stationed at the head of his party's Women's Division, to oversee appointments and serve as a general advisor on women's affairs. Truman placed no women in his cabinet, but, with the able assistance of India Edwards, he made other well-publicized appointments of women. Particularly notable were his designations of the first female ambassador, Eugenie Moore Anderson (Denmark), the first woman to sit on an independent regulatory commission, Frieda Hennock (Federal Communications Commission), and the first female Assistant Secretary of Defense, Anna Rosenberg. Advised by Bertha Adkins, Eisenhower also won favor with party women for his appointments, which were nearly as numerous as Roosevelt's. Best-known of these were Oveta Culp Hobby, who became Secretary of the newly created Department of Health, Education and Welfare, and Clare Booth Luce, Ambassador to Italy.

Party women encouraged appointments of women to lesser government positions as well, and while women did not exceed 2.4 percent of either President's appointees, a small-scale spoils system developed which provided at least token recognition of women party workers.[40] Women in both parties valued this limited but tangible evidence of their political power, and claimed the appointments attracted women's support and votes. Leaders of national women's organizations, recognizing the symbolic importance of these appointments, joined the party women in pressing for ever-larger numbers; they frequently drew up lists of women qualified for high-level appointments. The need for more women in government service was one of the few matters on which feminists and protectionists agreed.

While evidencing presidential concern for women, these appointments also served the less obvious function of absolving administrations from responsibility for further actions on women's behalf. Despite the mounting evidence of change in women's lives, presidents, party leaders, and public alike accepted the appointment of token women to government posts as an appropriate and sufficient recognition of women voters. The resulting limitation on women's political activities further crippled Women's Bureau efforts to draw attenion to the changing nature of women's roles. Significantly, it was party women, not WB Directors, who held access to the White House and thus spoke for and defined women's interests. Placing women in high posts was an admirable and important goal, but as Cynthia Harrison notes, it was of limited value as a strategy for advancing women's status.[41] The next chapter examines what happened when a new WB Director with access to the President began to implement a different strategy.

2

Peterson's Initiatives, 1960–1963

Equal employment opportunity for women began its development as a national policy during John F. Kennedy's presidency. Support for the principle was among the recommendations of the President's Commission on the Status of Women, which, from 1961 to 1963, investigated women's position in American society and drew up an agenda of desirable reforms. The Commission marks the beginning of governmental recognition of women's status as a legitimate matter for policy consideration. The Kennedy years also witnessed the first legislative recognition of federal responsibility toward working women, the Equal Pay Act of 1963. These initiatives were important steps in overcoming the attitudinal lag that thwarted the development of women's political issues in the preceding decades. Ironically, they were undertaken with the approval of a president whose record on behalf of women elicited severe criticism from women within his own party.

Both the initiatives and the criticism resulted from Kennedy's delegation of responsibility for women's affairs to Esther Peterson. By relying on one trusted woman to handle women's political concerns, Kennedy was continuing the practice of his predecessors. But while India Edwards and Bertha Adkins were primarily party women, Esther Peterson was a labor unionist. Her definition of women's interests and her strategy for advancing them emphasized educating public opinion and building legislative coalitions rather than securing appointments of women to high office. She also differed from many party women in her support of protective labor legislation, and consequent opposition to the Equal Rights Amendment. Because Peterson had access to Kennedy and the women at the Democratic National Committee did not, she was able to use her considerable political skills to persuade the federal government to begin dealing with the concerns of women, particularly those in the labor force.[1]

Peterson had a long-standing working relationship with Kennedy, dating from the time he sat on the House Labor Committee and she was a lobbyist for the Amalgamated Clothing Workers. She found Kennedy responsive to her legislative requests and worked congenially with him on such issues as minimum wage and unemployment insurance.[2] She joined his 1960 presidential campaign in its early stages and when Kennedy won the presidency, he offered Peterson her choice of jobs in his administration. Significantly, she chose Woman's Bureau Director. A knowledgeable politician with White House access, she brought a new prestige to the WB; her presence further increased the Bureau's status when Kennedy added Assistant Secretary of Labor to Peterson's title, increasing her duties and her authority.

Peterson hoped to use her post to effect a resolution of the ERA stalemate, thereby freeing women to unite in support of what she felt were more relevant concerns. A commission on the status of women was a key element of her strategy. The idea was not new; anti-ERA forces lobbied Congress for a commission in the 1940s and '50s, and in 1957 the National Manpower Council had also recommended a national commission to stimulate discussion of how U.S. "womanpower" might be employed to better advantage.[3] While Peterson envisioned a commission with broader concerns, her opposition to the ERA was an important motivation.

The ERA was a particularly sore point with Peterson. Kennedy's platform contained a plank endorsing "legislation which will guarantee to women equality of rights under the law."[4] Because it failed to mention a constitutional amendment, this statement was weaker than planks of previous years, but Peterson considered it an embarrassment for Kennedy because of his strong backing from organized labor, which opposed the ERA. Adding to Peterson's chagrin was Kennedy's personal endorsement of the amendment, which she believed the National Woman's Party secured by trickery. To Peterson, Kennedy's involvement with the ERA was a political mistake which he needed to rectify.[5]

Reflecting her labor union background, Peterson believed in "specific bills for specific ills." While the ERA purported to solve all women's legal problems, she contended it would actually solve very few. It would not, for example, help the large numbers of women working in trades which were exempted from the minimum wage coverage of the Fair Labor Standards Act. These women were the chief beneficiaries of state protective laws, which the ERA would invalidate. Peterson believed that such matters as extension of FLSA coverage and an equal pay law were more urgently needed and more attainable than the ERA.

Peterson's labor background also made her sensitive to the class interests involved in the debate. She was concerned that its proponents, relatively well-off professional women, had not given sufficient thought to its effect on less affluent women. Noting that such enemies of the labor movement as the National Association of Manufacturers, the National Association of Chambers of Commerce, and the American Retail Federation favored the ERA, Peterson later recalled that her opposition stemmed chiefly from mistrust of the ERA's supporters. The groups who opposed equal pay and minimum wage extension could not, she believed, be friends of working women.[6]

She hoped her proposed commission would move the discussion away from a Constitutional amendment into more fruitful areas. She was convinced that a fresh appraisal of women's status was necessary before women could begin to make political and economic progress. Backing from the energetic new President who promised to "get this country moving again" would make such an appraisal both possible and significant. How Peterson persuaded Kennedy and his staff to approve the commission is not clear. In a 1978 interview, she spoke of "struggles" and "fights" in getting her views accepted, but contended that Kennedy was sympathetic to her ideas.[7] Their long friendship was surely a factor, and Kennedy's endorsement of the ERA may have given Peterson some leverage.

Whatever his reasons for acceding, Kennedy's decision made political sense. The commission was admirably suited to give political recognition to a group whose status was changing. Although the ramifications of this change were immense (and potentially unsettling) for the entire society, the topic had attracted little political discussion, and no proper course of action was readily apparent. A presidential commission would encourage discussion, provide public input, and possibly suggest some course for the administration to follow in its treatment of women.[8] Less obviously, the commission would serve Kennedy much as token female appointees served his predecessors, obviating him of further responsibility for women's concerns. Having agreed to a commission, Kennedy apparently felt no need to pursue other means of recognizing women voters.

Party women disagreed. Kennedy's failure to appoint women to high office aroused complaints beginning in the earliest months of his presidency. In March, 1961, Eleanor Roosevelt called at the Whtie House to give the President a three-page list of women qualified for top government jobs. She explained to reporters afterward that men sometimes needed to be reminded that such women exist. Several other politically active women wrote letters of complaint to Kennedy. Emma Guffey Miller, a member of the Democratic National Committee and the NWP, expressed "grievous disappointment" that the few women Kennedy appointed were "merely replacing other women, while the important posts formerly filled by women are now being handed over to men." Director of the Mint Eva Adams suggested that Republicans could use Kennedy's slighting of women to advantage in the next campaign.[9]

Kennedy did make some female appointments, and in numerical terms, his record did not differ significantly from Eisenhower's or Truman's; in each administration, women held only 2.4 percent of all appointive posts. But Kennedy failed to place his female appointees in visible and noteworthy positions: there were no cabinet members, no "firsts," many Collectors of Customs. The appointments were not highly publicized, another change from past practice. Worse still, Kennedy failed to consult party women. They resented his break with tradition and their own loss of power.[10] But Kennedy took no conciliatory action, and criticism continued throughout his tenure. It must have been infuriating, especially to these women, that Kennedy never considered their complaints a serious political threat.

Peterson, the one political woman who had Kennedy's ear, did not press him for appointments; they were not relevant to her strategy, and she found more important matters on which to expend her political capital. One such issue concerned staffing the commission. When she approached Kennedy's staff on the selection of a chairman, an aide began the discussion: "Well, it can't be Mrs. Roosevelt!" Eleanor Roosevelt was who Peterson had in mind, although she knew the former First Lady and the new President regarded each other warily. Roosevelt, who led the Adlai Stevenson wing of the Democratic party, had not supported Kennedy in the 1960 primaries; although she campaigned for him in the general election, relations between the two were uneasy. Peterson argued, "You've got to have *the* best chairman or this won't amount to anything," and Kennedy acquiesced, on the condition that Peterson persuade her to accept the position.[11] Kennedy surely realized that Roosevelt's participation would increase his stature within the liberal wing of the party.

Eleanor Roosevelt was reluctant to accept the chairmanship; her health was poor, and she may have been hesitant about lending her name to a Kennedy undertaking. Yet advancing women's status was a cause to which she had a long-standing and serious commitment. As First Lady she had advocated a larger and more active role for women in politics and government, and she retained this special interest. She had also been a leading supporter of the anti-ERA proposal to establish a Congressional investigation of women's status. Because of her interest and Peterson's persuasive arguments, Roosevelt agreed to accept the chairmanship despite her ill health. She told Peterson prophetically, "This may be the last thing I ever do."[12]

To assure the commission's effectiveness, Peterson selected its members for their stature and influence rather than for their views on women or their political accomplishments. She sought business and labor leaders, educators, and cabinet members to fill the commission, believing that participation in its deliberations would educate them to the needs and problems of women. Then, after completing their work, they would be in a position to help carry out their own recommendations. Over one hundred persons were finally invited to participate, but only twenty-six were members of the commission itself. Six of these were cabinet members: the Attorney General, Chairman of the Civil Service Commission, and the Secretaries of Labor, HEW, Commerce, and Agriculture. Peterson credits Vice President Johnson with arousing cabinet interest and supporting her efforts to secure powerful members, but Johnson also prevailed upon her to make the one strictly political appointment to the commission for a friend of his from Texas.[13]

The other members met Peterson's criterion of influence, but their selection was designed to produce neither a balanced nor totally objective viewpoint. The large number of members representing labor and religious groups who opposed the ERA assured that the commission's statement on that important issue (and on other issues as well) would be acceptable to Peterson.[14]

Peterson deliberately chose nonpolitical members, and never considered using any of the commission slots to reward or recognize past accomplishments on women's behalf.[15] Yet India Edwards's absence generated criticism from party women, who felt Edwards's past accomplishments entitled her to membership. Interviewed in 1975, Edwards was still bitter. Apparently unaware of Peterson's rationale, or her key role in the selection process, Edwards blamed Kennedy's aides, the "Irish mafia," for her exclusion; they did not take political women seriously, she felt. While conceding that Kennedy himself had always treated her courteously, she remained convinced that he viewed women as "nothing but sex objects."[16] Whether justified or not, Edwards's criticisms circulated among Democratic women, exacerbating their bitterness towards Kennedy.

On December 14, 1961, Kennedy signed Executive Order 10980 establishing the President's Commission on the Status of Women (PCSW). The preamble to the Executive Order contained the public justification for the Commission and touched on the major themes that would be developed as the government groped toward a policy for women.

WHEREAS prejudices and outmoded customs act as barriers to the full realization of women's basic rights which should be respected and fostered as part of our Nation's commitment to human dignity, freedom, and democracy; and

WHEREAS measures that contribute to family security and strengthen home life will advance the general welfare; and

WHEREAS it is in the national interest to promote the economy, security, and national defense through the most efficient and effective utilization of the skills of all persons; and

WHEREAS in every period of national emergency women have served with distinction in widely varied capacities but thereafter have been subject to treatment as a marginal group whose skills have been inadequately utilized; and

WHEREAS women should be assured the opportunity to develop their capacities and fulfill their aspirations on a continuing basis irrespective of national exigencies; and

WHEREAS a Governmental Commission should be charged with the responsibility for developing recommendations for overcoming discriminations in government and private employment on the basis of sex and for developing recommendations for services which will enable women to *continue their roles as wives and mothers while making a maximum contribution to the world around them....*[17] (Emphasis added.)

The preamble's general terms glossed over any potential conflicts, e.g., between the basic rights of women, effective utilization of the nation's skills, and a strong family life. The document envisioned no revolutionary changes; it reinforced the concept of "woman's sphere" while implying that this sphere might be somewhat expanded. As Mary Eastwood of the Justice Department later commented, "the 'maximum contribution' contemplated for women was something less than an equal contribution."[18]

The Executive Order asked the members to "review progress and make recommendations as needed for constructive action" in seven specific areas. The Commission appointed seven Committees to study and report on these areas: Education, Home and Community, Civil and Political Rights, Social Insurance and Taxes, Protective Labor Legislation, Private Employment, and Federal Employment. Drawing recommendations from the Committee reports, the Commission hammered out a final unanimous report and presented it to President Kennedy on October 11, 1963.

Commission members viewed their task as a pioneering effort. Vice Chairman Richard A. Lester explained that the members wanted to "get as far as they could in areas where they could make a real difference." Accordingly, they sidestepped divisive issues and concentrated their efforts on matters for which corrective action was reasonably attainable and on which there was general agreement.[19] This strategy enabled the PCSW to achieve encouraging results in several areas even before it disbanded.

Participants were especially pleased with a reform they effected in federal hiring policy. While women comprised nearly one-fourth of federal employees, very few held positions at managerial or policy making levels. A Civil Service Commission (CSC) study, undertaken at the PCSW's request, found that federal employment of women differed little from that of private companies. The average grade of all federal women employees under the Classification Act was GS-4; for men the average was GS-9. Less than two percent of all positions at GS-13 and above were held by women.[20]

Just as the President's Committee on Equal Employment Opportunity (PCEEO), led by Vice President Johnson, was trying to make government employment of minorities a model for the nation's businesses, the PCSW hoped to make the federal government a "showcase" of employment opportunity for women. A policy of hiring and appointing women to upper-echelon positions would constitute a public affirmation of women's abilities, and at the same time, set an example for private employers to emulate. Johnson's PCEEO tried to persuade government agencies and holders of government contracts to pursue a course of "affirmative action" to seek out minority employees, and while most of its efforts were directed toward obtaining voluntary compliance, it did have some enforcement power. The PCSW was operating at a less advanced stage, and concentrated mainly on making suggestions and on removing an old legal barrier to government employment of women.

Women's position in the merit system had never been clearly defined. The Civil Service Act of 1883 established a merit system with qualifying examinations to determine those eligible for government jobs, but federal appointing officials were allowed to specify the sex of applicants to be considered. Authority to stipulate the gender of job applicants came, ironically, from an 1870 law permitting women to be hired at the same pay as men; this law was interpreted as a grant of discretionary power, allowing officials to specify the sex of applicants for a particular job.[21]

In 1919, Women in Industry Service, forerunner of the WB, complained that 60 percent of the civil service examinations excluded women. The CSC repsonded by opening all exams to members of either sex, but still allowed appointing officers to stipulate a sex preference. The WB opposed this practice until the Harding administration passed the Veteran's Preference Act, which added points to the exam scores of veterans seeking federal employment. Because a hiring system based on exam scores weighted in veterans' favor would discriminate against women in practice, the WB then sought to maintain the appointing officers' discretion to request women. This was, Mary Anderson believed, the only way to get *any* women appointed. The NWP, as might be expected, insisted on a strict merit basis for appointments. In 1932, Jessie Dell, head of the CSC and an NWP member, persuaded President Hoover to issue an Executive Order removing the appointing officers' discretion to specify sex, but this order lasted only one year: Mary Anderson got the newly elected Roosevelt to countermand it.[22]

When the PCSW explored the question, it found that appointing officers were using their discretion to specify males for nearly all professional and executive positions and for many lower-level jobs as well.[23] The Veteran's Preference Act was still in effect, but the number of veterans seeking federal jobs in the early 1960s was not the threat it had been following the World Wars and the Korean conflict. Allowing agencies to state a preference had not helped women; as long as appointing officers continued to request men, the policy only added to the discrimination against female applicants.

At the Commission's request, Attorney General Robert Kennedy examined the situation and issued a revised interpretation of the 1870 law. President Kennedy, as a result, ordered federal agencies to make appointments without regard to sex, except in special cases approved by the CSC.

The CSC established a requirement that agencies specifying a particular sex for a position must state their reasons for doing so. According to CSC Chairman John Macy, the requirement had a "a prompt effect. Virtually every subsequent request was submitted without a sex preference expressed." The President also directed Macy to "review pertinent personnel policies and practices affecting the employment of women," with a view towards eliminating other discriminatory practices.[24]

PCSW members were justifiably proud of this "breakthrough." Removing the sex specification option was a step toward equal employment opportunity for women, if only a small one. Such matters as training and promotion practices, job qualification standards, and the negative attitudes of federal managers continued to limit the numbers of women in the upper levels of the federal service. However, Kennedy's directive did mark the beginning of the government's efforts to evaluate its own record in providing equal employment opportunity for women.[25]

The PCSW achieved a similarly modest but important breakthrough by convincing the Defense Department to introduce legislation lifting restrictions on the number of female officers in the armed services.[26] Another area of agreement was federal equal pay legislation, and on this issue, too, the Commission saw progress during its life: President Kennedy signed the Equal Pay Act in June, 1963. The PCSW was not directly involved in the Equal Pay Act's passage, as it had been in securing CSC reforms or female officer's legislation. It endorsed the bill at its first meeting, but its biggest contributions came from the aura of legitimacy it gave to discussion of government policy for women.

Securing passage of an equal pay bill was another of Peterson's major goals, and she began organizing the means at her disposal shortly after arriving at the WB. The National Committee on Equal Pay, formed in 1952 (see Chapter 1), continued to function. Equal pay bills continued to be introduced in every session, but no hearings had been held since 1950. No one disputed the justice of the equal pay principle, but few politicians recognized an urgent problem. Esther Peterson reflected later that one of the greatest barriers to an equal pay law was the assumption, often unconscious, that women's work was not worth as much as men's.[27] This assumption related to the widely held notion that since women did not belong in the work force, any problems they experienced there were not important, a view the PCSW was challenging. Peterson's strategy for passing an equal pay bill involved gathering data proving a need for the bill and refuting the arguments used against it, then using that information to educate Congress.[28]

Opposition to equal pay bills came almost exclusively from business and manufacturing interests. They argued that federal legislation was unnecessary since market forces, backed by state equal pay laws, were already correcting inequalities in pay. Another argument, contradictory to the first, was that women had to be paid less since their higher turnover and absentee rates made them more costly to employ. An equal pay law might, therefore, cause employers to cease hiring women altogether, or at least force employers to segregate jobs still further so that men and women would not be doing the same work.[29]

Under Peterson's direction, the WB gathered information to refute these arguments. It found data which showed the differences in absenteeism and turnover between men and women to be quite small. The worker's age and the job's salary and status were more important variables than sex. Thus women's rates were slightly higher than men's because women held lower-paying and less important jobs. These findings indicated that women were not more costly to employ. With statistics showing that payment of lesser wages to women for equal work was a relatively common practice, and a study detailing the weak and ineffective nature of most state equal pay laws, the Bureau was able to assert that unequal pay was a problem for which existing solutions were inadequate. These specific findings gave a new trenchancy to arguments for federal equal pay legislation. They were added to the older, more general arguments that sex-related wage differentials were unjust, and adversely affected the economy by encouraging inefficient utilization of the work force and limiting purchasing power.[30]

Given the handicap imposed by lack of relevant broadscale research, the Bureau's arguments made an impressive case for a federal equal pay law. But the opposition's strong objections to increasing federal investigatory powers were not subject to statistical refutation, and remained a problem. Various proposals for enforcing the law included creating an Equal Pay Division within the WB, or delegating unspecified enforcement authority to the Secretary of Labor. Business groups opposed both, objecting to the expense of creating new enforcement machinery as well as to the potential for bureaucratic harassment.

Data gathering was the WB's specialty; lobbying was not. Peterson had to find other ways to get the WB's information to Congress. She claims that Kennedy's designation of the bill as an administration measure was crucial to its enactment, although such endorsement from previous administrations had never been sufficient. Peterson mentions Lyndon Johnson as a valuable ally, not only in helping her sell the bill to the White House, but also in planning strategy to get it through Congress.[31] Representative Edith Green (D., Ore.) was another important source of support. Green, a PCSW member, and long-time supporter of equal pay, sat on the House Committee on Education and Labor which held hearings on the bill.[32] But the person ultimately responsible for selling the bill to Congress was Morag Simchak, whom Peterson hired as a "technical assistant." Simchak's work was effective.[33]

In 1962 a bill passed both houses, but in different forms, and, because a technicality prevented it from going to conference, it died in the final days of the 87th Congress. The following year, Representative Charles Goodell (R., N.Y.) presented an equal pay bill which overcame the most serious objections of the business community. He proposed making equal pay an amendment to the Fair Labor Standards Act of 1938, thus using the already-established machinery of the Wage and Hour Division of the Department of Labor to enforce the law.

Realizing that this tactic would improve chances for passage and assure strong enforcement, supporters of equal pay adopted Goodell's idea. This change limited the coverage of the bill to those employees already covered by the FLSA, and meant that about two-thirds of the female work force would be exempt from its provisions.[34] Some of the poorest classes of workers— laundry, hotel, restaurant, and private household employees, farm workers, and employees of small retail establishments—were excluded, as well as those at the other end of the economic spectrum: administrative, executive and professional employees. Proponents of equal pay, like the PCSW members, believed the important point was to make a start. Once a bill was passed and the principle established, they could then work for extended coverage (which they did, successfully, in 1966 and 1972). Representative Edith Green incorporated Goodell's idea into a bill of her own, and Senator Pat McNamara (D., Mich.) presented a similar bill to the Senate. These bills were approved, and the Equal Pay Act was signed by President Kennedy on June 10, 1963.

Because the act applied only to those relatively few instances in which men and women performed the same work, it would not ease the gap between men's and women's overall earnings unless accompanied by equal access to jobs. But it was important as a policy statement that women's work was as valuable as men's. Broadened by later court interpretations to require equal pay for *substantially* equal work, the Act turned out to be more potent than its supporters had realized. Highly publicized court cases in which companies were forced to award large amounts of back pay to victims of discrimination drew public attention to wage disparities, and occasioned a fair amount of corrective action.[35] Using the established review and enforcement machinery of the Wage and Hour Division proved a boon, for effective enforcement was implemented within a relatively short period of time. Into the 1980s, the Equal Pay Act remained the best-enforced of the laws dealing with discrimination against women.

Short-term results of the Equal Pay Act were also impressive. The victory provided an immense psychological boost to women and organizations interested in advancing women's status. Added to the existence of the PCSW, the Equal Pay victory seemed to signal the dawn of a new political climate for women's issues.

A new interest was developing in several states where Governors had established commissions to investigate and make recommendations just as the PCSW was doing on the national level. Governors' Commissions on the Status of Women were promoted by the WB and by the National Federation of Business and Professional Women's Clubs. The WB sponsored several regional conferences to drum up interest, and Marguerite Rawalt, PCSW member and president of the BPW, led her organization in a lobbying campaign. By June 1964, twenty-one states had commissions on the status of women.[36]

The WB now appeared to have won the initiative in its long struggle with the National Woman's Party. NWP members had lobbied against the Equal Pay Bill, arguing that equal pay was useless without equal access to jobs, and that both could be guaranteed by the ERA. One NWP member later charged that the main effect of the Equal Pay Act had been to increase "job security for men by discouraging [their] replacement with lower paid women."[37] The Business and Professional Women, however, had joined with old-time WB allies such as the National Consumers' League, and the National Councils of Negro, Catholic, and Jewish Women to lobby for the Act.

American Women, the report of the PCSW, delivered in October, 1963, concurred with and reinforced the general philosophy of the WB. The report clearly accepted the concept of "women's sphere," stating:

> Widening the choices for women beyond their doorstep does not imply neglect of their education for responsibilities in the home. Modern family life is demanding, and most of the time and attention given to it comes from women.[38]

Yet the Commission also endorsed another long-held WB tenet that government should help women expand the "choices beyond their doorstep." Its recommendations for flexibly scheduled education and special counselling for women, for expanded and improved child care services, for increased part-time employment opportunities, and for paid maternity leaves, were based on the idea—and growing reality—that women held dual roles as wage earners and homemakers. *American Women* reflected the Commission's desire to educate the public on women's changing role, and to initiate the process of formulating public policy to deal with women's changing status. The report viewed the role of public policy not so much as an instrument of change in itself, but more as a means of facilitating and rationalizing changes that were already occurring. This was a repudiation, whether intentional or not, of the NWP philosophy.

American Women made no definitive statement on the Equal Rights Amendment. According to Vice Chairman Richard Lester, a serious discussion of the ERA would have badly split the PCSW, and since there was little to be gained from a bitter debate, the Commission settled the issue by temporizing.[39]

Realizing that dissension over this issue was a major hurdle to women's progress, Commission members worked hard to secure an accommodation that both sides could support.[40] A brief prepared by Pauli Murray of Yale Law School suggested a strategy for developing constitutional recognition of women's rights without an amendment. Murray argued that the due process clause of the Fifth Amendment and the equal protection clause of the Fourteenth could be interpreted to guarantee equal treatment of the sexes before the law. The catch, of course, lay in persuading the courts to accept an interpretation so contrary to precedent. The Supreme Court, as the NWP was fond of pointing out, had consistently held that sex was a valid basis for legal classification. A carefully worded statement based on Murray's brief extricated the Commission from a delicate position. It did not repudiate the ERA; indeed, it accepted a major premise of the amendment's proponents:

> Equality of rights under the law for all persons, male or female, is so basic to democracy ... that it must be reflected in the fundamental law of the land.

Yet by arguing that legal equality between the sexes was already embodied in the Constitution, the Commission was able to conclude that "a constitutional amendment need not *now* be sought in order to establish this principle." [Emphasis added.] This satisfied proponents of protective labor legislation, who believed judicial reinterpretation of the Fifth and Fourteenth Amendments would not disturb these laws. The word "now" in the statement, added at the request of Marguerite Rawalt, left open the possibility of pursuing an amendment if Murray's strategy did not bring the desired response from the Courts. The report urged that test cases be submitted for court review. The PCSW did not resolve the old debate, but by temporizing on this issue, it cleared the way for action on other fronts.[41]

Protective labor laws, which played a key role in the old ERA debate, were the only other subject of major contention. Participants agreed on the ultimate goal: strongly enforced labor standards applying to workers of both sexes. The Committee on Protective Labor Legislation, however, feared that an immediate push towards this ultimately desirable goal might slow the development or extension of protection to additional women. Realizing that these laws might overprotect women in executive, administrative or professional positions, the Committee agreed that these categories should be exempt. But it argued that women's protective laws, particularly those limiting hours of work, still served a special function: since women were clustered in occupations which tended not to be unionized, many women workers had no defense against exploitation other than that supplied by statute. Committee member Mary Dublin Keyserling, a former officer of the National Consumers' League, held strongly protectionist views which influenced the committee.[42] Later, as Johnson's WB Director, she would continue to support laws only for women and would do so against increasing opposition. In 1963, her views prevailed. The Commission's final recommendation supported the principle of labor standards for all workers, but added, "Until such time as this goal is attained, state legislation limiting maximum hours of work for women should be maintained, strengthened, and expanded."[43] Unlike its ERA statement, which was more nearly a compromise, *American Women's* position on protective laws locked the WB even more tightly into the philosophy it had followed since its creation. Extending and strengthening protections for women, however necessary, forestalled the development of sex-neutral labor legislation. The statement was, in any case, congruent with the general philosophy of the Commission that women's roles in the home made them unique.

Despite that philosophy, many of the Commission's recommendations were designed to facilitate women's advancement in the labor market. PCSW members recognized that equal employment opportunity for women was crucial to this advancement, but their recommendations for achieving it were tempered by their interpretation of the limits of political possibility. The Commission considered equal employment opportunity under three classifications: (1) federal employment, for which the possiblity of corrective action was greatest; (2) private employment, for which any sort of coercive antidiscrimination legislation appeared unrealistic; and (3) employment by private businesses holding government contracts, for which there was some precedent for federal intervention.

The PCSW made some gains in the area of federal employment. The Attorney General's ruling and consequent CSC reforms would help equalize opportunities for women within the civil service, and the Commission's statement on women appointees envisioned "increasing consideration" for women's services at the policy making level of government as well.[44]

On the subject of private employment, the Commission apparently never considered the possibility of coercive federal legislation. It rejected a modest recommendation from its Committee on Civil and Political Rights for a study of the "need for and desirability of Federal and State affirmative legislation to remove discrimination in employment."[45]

American Women lumped the Commission's recommendation on private employment together with an equally weak statement on employment by government contractors:

> Equal opportunity for women in hiring, training, and promotion should be the governing principle in private employment. An Executive order should state this principle and advance its application to work done under Federal contracts.[46]

This recommendation was based on the report of the Commission's Committee on Private Employment, which engaged in considerable debate on the matter. Government enforcement of nondiscriminatory hiring policies for private businesses did not appear to be a tenable position, but there was ample precedent for a stronger statement on the employment policies of government contractors, and some Committee members advocated one.

Businesses holding government contracts had been subject to federal oversight of their hiring policies since 1941 when President Roosevelt issued an Executive Order creating the Fair Employment Practices Committee. Succeeding presidents established their own committees to encourage government contractors to hire and promote employees without discrimination on the basis of race, creed, color or national origin. These efforts, including the PCEEO headed by Vice President Johnson, had never been noted for their strength, and had undergone persistent criticism from both conservatives and civil rights advocates, who argued that the committees were either meddlesome or ineffective. Yet they had achieved some results, and their existence provided a slightly-more-than-symbolic national policy of antidiscrimination. Some members of the Committee on Private Employment advocated an Executive Order establishing a similar body with enforcement powers to insure that federal funds did not support companies which flagrantly discriminated against their female employees.

Caroline Davis of the United Auto Workers suggested an even stronger approach: amending the Executive Order governing the PCEEO to include sex. Her suggestion was rejected because

> The consensus was that the nature of discrimination on the basis of sex and the reasons for it are so different [from the nature of and reasons for racial discrimination] that a separate program is necessary.[47]

Backed by the support of the UAW for her position, Davis prepared a "Dissent" which was published along with the Committee's Report. "The history of our society," Davis wrote,

> records at least a hundred years of experience in programs based upon voluntary compliance with the ideals and policies which we as a democratic nation espouse. One has only to reflect upon the plight of minority groups with respect to voting rights, equal access to education, housing, and apprenticeable trades, in addition to employment opportunities, before and even after the rulings by the Attorney General and the decisions of the Supreme Court, in order to understand the need for strong prohibitive language and enforcement provisions if we are to fulfill the worthy objectives of providing equal opportunity to women working for employers holding Government contracts.

Assuring equity to these women who are, incidently, taxed equally to support the defense program of this country, is a matter of simple justice, economic good sense, and moral obligation.[48]

Citing its reasons for choosing a voluntary approach rather than one with legal enforcement provisions, the Committee on Private Employment stressed the spirit of cooperation that could be developed in working out a solution to the problem. Richard Lester, who headed the Committee, privately gave the more understandable reason that it did not believe a stronger position could be accepted or enforced.[49]

Such compromises were tolerable because *American Women* would not be the last word on the subject of women's status. The Commission proposed a means to allow continuation and expansion of its efforts. Its final recommendation asked the President to establish an ongoing commission of executive department and agency heads under the supervision of a Cabinet officer, and a complementary advisory committee of private citizens. Both were to meet periodically and report to the President on further means of advancing women's status. These continuing bodies would foster implementation of the PCSW's recommendations and perhaps eventually reevaluate the moderate stance taken on such issues as equal employment opportunity.

The occasion for a reevaluation came, as Esther Peterson noted wryly, "more rapidly than most people had anticipated," when equal employment opportunity for women became part of the debate over the Civil Rights Act of 1964.[50] (See Chapter 4.) The issue of an Executive Order to forbid sex discrimination by government contractors would surface again too. (See Conclusion.) But before this, Kennedy was assassinated in the home state of his Vice President.

On the day following the assassination, as the nation reeled at the shock of Kennedy's death, and eulogies were the order of the day, Anna Rosenberg Hoffman told a reporter that there were "far fewer women in important political positions today than during the Roosevelt and Truman administrations."[51] Hoffman, formerly known as Anna Rosenberg, was a public figure; her criticism was thus particularly biting. She would soon share her thoughts on the matter with the new President.

Kennedy had been aware of the criticism. In July 1963, Clayton Fritchey, a long-time party professional, spoke to him about it, stressing the fact that women comprised a majority of the electorate, and were becoming increasingly involved in politics. Fritchey argued that a few notable appointments would silence the small but persistent group of complainers and win widespread support for the administration as well. Kennedy was sufficiently interested to ask Fritchey to send him a memo on the subject. "Currently," Fritchey wrote, we not only have no Mrs. Roosevelt but no Madam Perkins, or Anna Rosenberg, or India Edwards, whose names became household words in previous Democratic regimes. Even the Eisenhower regime had its Clare Luce and Oveta Hobby. Today there are no really famous women serving the Government. But, perhaps even more important, there are few in positions that would tend to make them famous. It would not take many appointments to create a favorable impression if (1) the jobs were significant and (2) the appointees were noteworthy personalities.[52]

Fritchey's analysis would seem to be a compelling argument, more so than the complaints of a few cantankerous party workers, for Kennedy to make at least one major appointment of a woman. There were no political risks involved, and the possibility of gaining support certainly existed. Kennedy, however, chose not to act on Fritchey's advice in the remaining few months of his life.

Kennedy shared society's reservations about working women. When Eleanor Roosevelt, interviewing him for a television program in 1962, asked Kennedy why there were so few women in top government positions, he commented that childrearing interrupted women's lives and prevented them from acquiring skills.

... the problem of how a mother can meet her responsibilities to her children and at the same time contribute to society in general, is the most sensitive and important matter, and... I am interested in what your [the PCSW's] suggestions would be.[53]

Kennedy used the Commission to temporize on the matter of female appointments, and since the Commission report came just six weeks before his death, he was neither forced nor permitted to consider the matter further. Yet by following Esther Peterson's strategy, he made a significant contribution to the development of national policy for women. The Commission he appointed and supported constituted an acknowledgment of women's problems and suggested a federal role in their solution. The long-range implications of that fact made the appointment issue appear trivial.

3

Affirmative Action from the
White House, 1964

Less than two months after his sudden accession to the Presidency, Lyndon Johnson initiated a campaign to put more women in top government jobs. He promised to place at least fifty women in policy making positions, and pressured cabinet members and heads of executive agencies to promote women to the upper grades of the civil service. An affirmative action reporting system for women, surely the first of its kind, was established in the White House at Johnson's direction. Under this system, aides pressed departments and agencies for action, kept a count of the numbers of women appointed and promoted, and maintained a list of women qualified for government service.

In a series of speeches designed to publicize the campaign, Johnson pledged an end to "stag government" and reminded the country that it could not afford to waste half of its human resources. He hoped his example would inspire leaders in business, industry, and the professions to throw off "outmoded prejudices" and seek ways to utilize women's talents more fully.

Johnson's campaign on behalf of women was consonant with his personal beliefs and with his idea of the national interest. His vision of a strong, prosperous country with an ever-expanding economic base—what he would later call the Great Society—required the rational development and use of human resources, including women. His experience in working with political women convinced him it was possible and desirable, as well as necessary, for women to play a greater role in the economic and political life of the nation. But his effort to put more women in government service was motivated chiefly by his peculiar political situation. Once that situation changed, his personal attention to his campaign waned. Major appointments of women never reached fifty, and the reporting system was demoted from the White House to the Interdepartmental Committee on the Status of Women.

Yet Johnson's actions and words had implications beyond the matter of appointments. He singled out women as a group worthy of policy consideration, and called national attention to the fact of sex discrimination in the workplace at a time when solutions to the problem of racially discriminatory hiring practices were being hotly debated in Congress and around the country. He also bestowed importance on the initiatives of the President's Commission on the Status of Women. By acting on one of its major recommendations and implying support for other measures to upgrade women's status, he created a climate in which further action was possible.

When the new President announced his intention to put fifty women in top government jobs, columnist Charles Bartlett remarked, "It's ridiculous. A President ought to spend more time on policy than on public relations stunts."[1] The campaign to put more women in government was undoubtedly a public relations stunt, executed in what would come to be known as typical Johnson style. It featured hyperbole, grandiose promises, attempts to bedazzle the press, and an emphasis on numbers that seemed somehow deceptive. The campaign was, nevertheless, a declaration of policy. Columnist Bartlett, along with most Americans, was not willing to accept the idea that statements about women's employment could constitute "policy," but to the women who had complained about the small number of Kennedy's female appointees, Johnson's words signalled an important and welcomed policy change.

For the President, the women in government campaign was a method of dealing with his peculiar political circumstances. Upon taking office in November, 1963, Johnson had two overwhelming concerns: to provide continuity and stability to the government, and to assure his own election in less than a year. Both tasks presented a challenge to Johnson's political skills, for he was not a nationally known figure, and the inevitable comparisons with Kennedy did nothing to enhance his image.

Kennedy, with his youth, physical attractiveness, and charisma, had become a romantic and glamorous symbol of a hoped-for new era, and his assassination evoked a sense of bewilderment and loss in the United States and throughout the world. He had not been particularly successful as President: his legislative program was stalled in Congress, largely because of opposition from the Southern wing of his own party, and his diplomatic efforts had brought marked improvement neither in Cold War tensions nor in the U.S. position *vis á vis* the U.S.S.R. Kennedy nevertheless enjoyed immense popularity that increased with his death.

By comparison, Johnson appeared crude and homely. He lacked Kennedy's wit, urbanity, and educational credentials, and his Texas drawl presented a noticeable contrast to Kennedy's more fashionable Boston accent. Kennedy's staff referred to him as "Uncle Cornpone." Because Johnson had been chosen as the vice presidential nominee in 1960 to "balance the ticket," Kennedy's supporters felt an instinctive distrust of him. His political ties to Texas oil interests and conservative Southern Democrats, and his reputation as a back-room, arm-twisting politician only increased their suspicions.

Outside of Washington and Texas, Lyndon Johnson was not known. He had no national base of support and little recognition among the general public. During his twenty-six years in Congress and his term as Senate Majority Leader, he purposely avoided the limelight, building his power base in the Senate rather than among the public. Nor was he well known in foreign capitals. That Kennedy and his alleged assassin Oswald had both been murdered in Johnson's home state exacerbated Johnson's problems in reassuring the United States and the world that the government would continue to operate effectively.

Given these circumstances, it seems natural that Johnson would choose to wrap himself in Kennedy's mantle. While stressing the continuity of the Democratic administration, Johnson would be able to use his considerable legislative talents to pass the measures that Kennedy had articulated but failed to secure. This legislation centered chiefly on items which had been part of the public debate for nearly a decade: civil rights, federal aid to education, health care for the aged—matters which were still controversial but upon which a national consensus was building.[2]

Assuming from his observations of past administrations that he would have a "honeymoon" period with the Congress, Johnson could feel reasonably assured of some legislative success. But he also realized that passing Kennedy's legislation would not build him the kind of support he would need for election in 1964; he wanted large chunks of the electorate to feel loyalty to Lyndon Johnson, not simply to the memory of John Kennedy. He had to find ways of distinguishing himself from Kennedy while remaining faithful to his memory, and he had to make sure that everyone knew about them. Public relations was thus an area of intense and justifiable concern to him. The security and well-being of the nation, and his own ability to lead it could, he believed, best be served by his rapidly, effectively, and visibly establishing a commanding presidential image of himself.

Almost immediately upon assuming office, Johnson began contacting the "natural leaders of the nation," asking for advice and support. During his first month in office, he visited with and telephoned hundreds of influential people. He spoke to governors, congressmen, and the three living former Presidents; he met with business, labor, civil rights, and religious leaders. Johnson tried to impress upon these leaders the importance of maintaining a strong, united posture in the world, of keeping the country's morale high, of moving ahead to meet the country's social and economic problems. The consensus he was attempting to forge was clearly in the nation's best interests, and what was good for the country was doing no harm to Johnson's own political fortunes.[3]

One of the people whom Johnson called upon for help was Anna

Rosenberg Hoffman, and it was she who persuaded him that the poor utilization of women's talents was a situation in need of correction and worthy of presidential attention. Hoffman was a shining example of what Johnson liked to call a "can do" woman.[4] During her high school days in New York, she organized her class to work for the suffrage amendment, and before she was herself old enough to vote, she managed the successful election campaign of a Tammany alderman. At the age of nineteen, she arbitrated her first labor dispute, beginning a successful career as a labor negotiator and public relations consultant.[5]

She became heavily involved in New Deal politics as a fund raiser, organizer, and sometime political advisor to President Roosevelt. Hoffman made a much needed contribution of $500 to Lyndon Johnson's first Congressional campaign in 1937 because a mutual friend advised her that Johnson was a "real liberal" and a supporter of FDR. Hoffman says that Johnson "never forgot," and in later years he several times publicly acknowledged his debt to her.[6]

In 1950, at the request of Secretary of Defense George C. Marshall, President Truman appointed her Assistant Secretary of Defense for Manpower; she was the first woman to hold such a post. As Assistant Secretary she made numerous appearances before the Senate's Armed Services Committee, of which Johnson was then a member. While often placed in an adversary relationship, Hoffman and Johnson developed a deep mutual respect.[7]

Johnson telephoned Hoffman for advice shortly after becoming President, and was sufficiently intrigued by what she said to request that she meet with him at the White House for further discussion.[8] On January 16, 1964, Hoffman and Johnson met for about half an hour.[9] Hoffman later told reporters that she and Johnson discussed "automation and the better utilization of women in the business and government world."[10] Her point about utilizing women in government obviously met with approval. The idea was Hoffman's but its implementation was purely Johnson's.

Later that day Liz Carpenter, Mrs. Johnson's Press Secretary, was waiting for the White House elevator when the President stepped off, grabbed her by the shoulder, and said, "Anna Rosenberg Hoffman tells me that we need more women in government. Get hold of Esther Peterson and be at the Cabinet meeting tomorrow."[11]

Reflecting on the speed with which Johnson acted on Hoffman's advice, Carpenter later recalled that Johnson was

> an impromptu man, who, when he saw somebody, remembered something that might have been on his desk. . .an idea that might have been under the surface for a long time, but this looked like the time to make it move.[12]

Hoffman's suggestion was the immediate cause of Johnson's actions, but as Carpenter's remarks indicate, the idea of advancing women was one to which Johnson was philosophically receptive, and which, in political terms, he found both appealing and timely.

As Vice President, Johnson had been aware of the resentment against Kennedy's lukewarm attitude toward female appointees. Early in 1961, Johnson's friend and advisor James Rowe alerted him to the

> tremendous and quiet criticism all over the country about the extremely small number of women who have been appointed, particularly in light of the fact that they are the ones who do most of the work.[13]

Johnson's contacts with the PCSW members, whom he and Mrs. Johnson entertained at their home, and his friendship with India Edwards, one of the chief complainers, surely reinforced his awareness.

Kennedy's Commission on the Status of Women had stressed the importance of having women appointed to high government posts, arguing that the federal government, in its capacity as an employer, should serve as a model to the private sector.[14] The fact that Kennedy had not acted on the PCSW's recommendation, which he received six weeks before going to Dallas, left Johnson free to make his own decision on this matter.

Johnson thus had a unique opportunity to surpass Kennedy by moving swiftly in an area where Kennedy had dragged his feet. The issue of placing more women in government was tailor-made for Johnson's situation. It provided an opportunity for him to appear decisive and presidential. It might become a source of favorable publicity. It would surely win him loyal support from the women who had been complaining. Johnson apparently believed, along with James Rowe, that women did "most of the work" in political campaigns, and he was eager to have female help in the upcoming campaign.

There were broader political gains to be won, as well, in the event that Johnson's actions sparked interest among women voters. Women were believed generally to prefer Republican candidates and to have favored Nixon in the 1960 election. They were thus, theoretically, a logical group for Democrats to court.[15]

Every president since Roosevelt felt compelled to make at least limited overtures toward women voters, but none became so personally involved with a woman's issue as did Johnson. The uncertainty of his political situation in early 1964, and his desperate desire for loyal supporters are sufficient explanations for his involvement.

Yet personal convictions as well as political calculations played a role in Johnson's willingness to promote Hoffman's ideas. Within his own family,

Johnson had two potent examples of women who belied the passive/ helpless stereotype so often associated with women. His mother, Rebekah Baines Johnson, was a strong-willed and forceful person who, with her college education and literary pretensions, appears to have felt culturally isolated in the small-town Texas of the early twentieth century. She adjusted to her situation by coaching the high school debating team, giving elocution lessons in her home, directing plays at the local opera house, and exerting intense pressure on her eldest son Lyndon to "make something" of himself.[16]

Johnson's wife, Lady Bird, was also an active and capable woman. She participated in Johnson's political campaigns, served as his "best advisor," and managed a lucrative radio and television business in Austin which provided the chief source of income for the family. Johnson often credited his wife for his interest in promoting women's status. He told reporters that she was constantly asking him, "What have you done for women today?"[17]

Yet any pressure she may have exerted was applied privately. She used the First Lady's power to attract publicity with consummate skill, directing the nation's attention to the plight of families in poverty, the importance of preserving wilderness areas, and various means of beautifying the landscape. She undertook campaigns and projects of her own, but in all her activities she projected an intense loyalty for, and unity of purpose with, her husband.

Promoting women's status was not one of her major public concerns, but she did attempt to secure dignified publicity for the constructive contributions women made to society. On the day of Hoffman's visit to the White House, Mrs. Johnson held the first in a series of luncheons for "Women Doers," giving public recognition to women who had achieved distinction in various fields.[18] These luncheons highlighted the achievement of famous women such as actress Helen Hayes, and less recognized good works, such as those of some New York women who arranged good will tours of the U.S. for delegates to the United Nations. The luncheons were an oblique and noncontroversial way of saying "remember the women," and did not attract widespread attention,[19] but they did offer recognition to some otherwise unsung heroines, and stressed Mrs. Johnson's belief that women's work was important.

Johnson himself had coined the term "women doers," presumably to denote the female counterpart to the "can do" man, a term he used as a high compliment.[20] Ability to get the job done was, for Johnson, a politician's most important attribute, and the fact that he had known and associated with numerous "women doers" was an important factor in his willingness to pursue Hoffman's idea.

Johnson came to Washington during the New Deal years, as women were making their first notable advances in political and government work. Several of his friendships with political women date from his early days as a

Congressman. Throughout his career, Johnson had worked with political women, and counted a number of them as his friends. Elizabeth Wickenden Goldschmidt, India Edwards, Libby Rowe, Helen Gahagan Douglas, Esther Peterson and Anna Rosenberg Hoffman had all worked with him on various political causes, and he respected their political know-how and capacity for hard work.[21] These working relationships, coupled with his aversion to theorizing, led Johnson to think in pragmatic terms of what he could do for women now, as opposed to Kennedy's more philosophical questioning of women's proper roles.

Johnson's admiration for former President Roosevelt may also have contributed to his willingness to open more doors to women in government service. Roosevelt went out of his way to help women advance in government service, but he and his successors moved cautiously into the domains of department and agency heads, allowing them a veto on women's appointments.[22] Johnson moved more forcefully; he began by applying personal pressure to his Cabinet.

It met on January 17, the day after Hoffman's visit. Carpenter and Peterson were present as requested. Following a brief lecture about economizing on government publications, Johnson turned to the "more pleasant" subject of women in government. Referring to the PCSW's finding that the "brainpower of American women" needed to be utilized at the "highest policy level," Johnson said, "I want every manager in government. . .to take note of this untapped resource. . . . [t]he day is over when the top jobs are reserved for men."[23]

He introduced Esther Peterson, who spoke for about twenty-five minutes on the lack of opportunities for women to advance in government service, and of the advantages of using the skills of trained women.[24]

Johnson warmed to the topic, and, departing from his agenda, continued to explain to the Cabinet that there were plenty of able women being overlooked. Carpenter recalls:

> He was looking at the Cabinet members. . . saying, "In the baskets on your desks, if you'll go back and look, you'll find there are a lot of women who've been asking for elevation. I want you to go back and see if we can't get some of them moving." And he got more and more enthusiastic about it, and said, "Report back to me next week how many you have placed." These were the magic words.[25]

Later the same day, Johnson repeated his "hire women" message to the directors of twenty independent and regulatory agencies who met with him at the White House.[26] Once again, Johnson delivered an impassioned lecture. Esther Peterson, who also attended this meeting, discreetly described Johnson's performance as "forceful," telling reporters that after he had spoken she found little that remained to be said.[27]

Press reports gave a more colorful version of the meeting. At one point, Johnson was said to have put two different agency directors on the spot by pointing a finger at them and demanding, "Do you have any women in top jobs in your agency?"[28] Becoming increasingly enthusiastic, Johnson told the assembled directors the story of how the women in his family secured his election to the Senate in 1948.[29] Shortly before the crucial primary election, Johnson related, he had become ill, and, weary of campaigning, had taken to his bed. But his wife, mother, and sister refused to give up campaigning. Gathering friends and relatives, they formed a party to call every name in the San Antonio telephone directory, asking each person to vote for Johnson. He won the election by 87 votes. This was one of his favorite stories about women, and he told it frequently, always adding, "This is the kind of stick-to-it-iveness we need in public life."

Critics at the time, and since, have attributed "Landslide Lyndon's" 1948 victory to less ennobled forms of campaigning; charges of various forms of election rigging continued to surface even after Johnson's death.[30] But concerning the point of the story, the President was apparently sincere. His public remarks indicate a belief that women, given the right opportunities, would out-perform men. Including more women in government, he declared, would make government more effective and more efficient. His orders to the Cabinet and agency heads to report to him their appointments and promotions of women underscored his seriousness.

Press coverage of the campaign to hire and promote women in government was crucial to its success, for it would put pressure on the officials responsible for hiring and give Johnson the publicity he desired. The press carried reports of the Cabinet and agency meetings, but the stories were short, and, in the Washington press, were placed chiefly on the women's pages.[31] Two weeks later, with the help of Isabelle Shelton, a reporter for the *Washington Evening Star*, Johnson got front page coverage for his campaign by dramatically setting a goal and timetable for himself.

Shelton was one of several female reporters whom the President had shown around the Oval Office shortly after moving in.[32] He extended the group a polite and indefinite invitation to "come back and talk to me sometime."[33] After learning of his remarks to the Cabinet and agency directors, Shelton asked Liz Carpenter to help her secure an interview with the President so that she could write a "lengthy and serious piece" about the President's feelings on helping women advance in the government. Carpenter passed Shelton's request along to the President, adding that a personal interview "would get you a lot of mileage."[34]

Meeting with Shelton on January 25, Johnson startled her by pledging that his administration would appoint fifty women to top government jobs within the following month. He talked about the women whose abilities he especially respected, mentioning his wife, his mother, Esther Peterson, Liz Carpenter, former U.S. Representative Helen Gahagan Douglas, Senators Maurine Neuberger and Margaret Chase Smith, and Oveta Culp Hobby, the Houston newspaper publisher and former Secretary of HEW for Eisenhower. He continued, expansively, on the importance of women in politics:

> They win our elections for us. We men stand around smoking cigars and say, "Somebody's got to go out to the precincts." Then we send our wives.[35]

Shelton's story, headlined "Johnson to Put 50 Women in Top Government Jobs," appeared on the front page of the *Star* on January 29. It explained that the number 50 had been determined by assuming one appointment for each of the approximately fifty executive departments and agencies. Top jobs were defined as "up to and including Under Secretaries, Assistant Secretaries, and Deputy Heads of agencies."

The President's search for talented women appointees, Shelton related, reflected his intention to "make the upgrading of women in American life one of the major goals of his administration." He hoped that his actions would eventually influence attitudes in private industry and the professions, opening more opportunities for women. The article included a quotation from the President:

> Women have the stickability, courage, and never-say-die attitude that you don't find in a man. They never give up when they believe something deeply. And they have the imagination, initiative and ingenuity that I like.[36]

Shelton's story, as intended, aroused interest. Upon questioning from reporters, a White House press aide confirmed the story "except for details." The aide would not commit the President to fifty appointments by the target date, but said the report was "substantially accurate."[37]

How carefully the President had considered his pledge before making it is hard to determine. There is no available evidence to suggest he discussed it with anyone beforehand, and it would not be out of character for this "impromptu" man to have thought of the idea while talking to Isabelle Shelton. Even if he failed to meet his goal, some women would be appointed, and he could reasonably expect a friendly voice to point out that he had done more than any previous president to help women advance in government service. The idea was flamboyant, and smacked of gimmickry, but more sober and carefully reasoned pleas in the past had not attracted much attention. Nor had years of general agreement that there ought to be more women in government made much change in the numbers of women in policy positions.

Shelton's story suggested that "some government experts" doubted the feasibility of placing so many women in upper level posts in such a short time. In reply, Shelton quoted a White House staff member: "When Lyndon B. Johnson says he wants it done in a month, it can be done." But not even Lyndon B. Johnson could overcome all the difficulties.

The first problem was to find fifty jobs. At the start of his presidency, Johnson requested Kennedy's appointees and staff to continue in their jobs.[38] Aside from his desire to show continuity with the Kennedy administration, Johnson's request was both astute and necessary; to have asked for resignations would have been unseemly, and Johnson did not have time to select his own people. As a consequence, he lacked the usual presidential prerogatives concerning appointments. Most government jobs, moreover, are not "top level" by any reasonably stringent definition, and in times of normal turnover, large numbers of policy making positions are not vacant.

Secondly, the pool from which women appointees could be selected was much smaller than that for males. While there was a substantial number of highly educated women with administrative and policy making ability, many of them lacked the political experience and "connections" necessary to political success. Compounding the problem was the fact that many qualified women were not anxious to become public servants; Johnson complained publicly that several women had turned down his offers.[39]

It has never been easy for the government to attract the best qualified males for a given position; government service for these people usually means accepting a drastic reduction in income, forfeiting the security of their jobs, and uprooting their families for a temporary stay in Washington. Thus the standard by which political appointments had been made was "the best man available" rather than the "best man for the job."[40] The consequences of accepting a political appointment would be even more threatening to a successful woman, for, being an anomaly, she had no assurance of finding another suitable job when her service was over. A married woman was faced with special difficulties in accepting a job that required her moving to Washington. If, as was usually the case, her husband could not or would not leave a job which provided a substantial part of the family's income, she had to go to Washington alone. As Betty Furness, one of Johnson's later appointees, said, "That is not the way our society is made up."[41] Liz Carpenter, who remained on the lookout for appointable women throughout her White House tenure, agreed. "The outstanding business or professional woman who is free to take a full time government job is still unique." she said.[42]

The task of prodding the executive branch to find these unique women, and of keeping records of any appointments and promotions fell to Special Assistant to the President Ralph Dungan, who had handled appointments for Kennedy. After checking with each agency and department on its progress, Dungan sent first weekly, and later biweekly, reports to the President.[43] These reports were designed to maximize numbers. They included appointments that were made before the campaign to find fifty women had begun, and many appointments that were not "top level" by any stretch of the imagination.

A report released to the press on February 27, at the end of the thirty days, listed 76 new appointments and promotions; yet the bulk of these (46 promotions and six appointments) were in grades GS 14 and 15, jobs with substantial salaries and responsibilities, but not "key" policy making posts.[44] Fourteen of the appointees became members of the Defense Advisory Committee on Women in the Services, an already established, all female group which functioned more as a means of creating political support for Defense Department policies than as an advisory committee.[45] Five appointees became members of the Annual Assay Commission, a group which met one day a year to check the silver content of U.S. coins.

Of the remaining five appointments, only one had the potential of being a policy making position; this was the newly created post of Special Assistant to the President for Consumer Affairs, to which Johnson had named Esther Peterson early in January before initiating his "campaign." Since Peterson already held two other key positions (Director of the Woman's Bureau and Assistant Secretary of Labor) this appointment did not increase the actual numbers of women in high posts, nor did it make administrative sense. No one questioned her energy or capability, but Peterson herself admitted that her job as Consumer Affairs assistant left her little time to devote to her other duties.[46]

Reviewing Johnson's appointments at the end of the thirty days, Isabelle Shelton concluded that he had set too tight a time limit, explaining that the necessary paperwork and security clearances slowed the announcement of appointments. Shelton predicted that more announcements would be forthcoming.[47] They were.

Even after the thirty day limit expired, Johnson appeared to be in a hurry to announce more appointments. He responded to bureaucratic delays by choosing to ignore some of the finer points of appointment protocol. He announced appointments of at least two women before they had accepted the posts offered them.[48] Two ambassadors were named without identifying the countries in which they would serve because the two countries had not yet been extended the diplomatic courtesy of a chance to approve the President's choices.[49]

During March and April, Johnson continued to push his campaign to end "stag government." At a meeting with the Joint Chiefs of Staff, a stronghold of male supremacy, he asked for reports on the numbers of women assigned to positions of responsibility.[50] At several news conferences he gave the latest figures on female appointments.[51] In speeches to the Women's National Press Club, the League of Women Voters, the Defense Advisory Committee on Women in the Service, and a Campaign Conference of Democratic Women, he spoke of his hopes to end the "waste of woman-power."[52]

At a White House reception honoring 150 new women appointees, Johnson made the most cogent presentation of his rationale. Noting that "Providence has distributed brains and skills pretty evenly over our people," Johnson said,

> We need skill and intelligence and capacity for leadership. We need dedication and application and we need them wherever we find them. If we neglect these talents, our society is the first loser.
>
> But equally, the women whose gifts are suppressed and passed over are losers, too. And in our open democratic society, the frustration of any of our citizens is a source of loss to all our citizens. All too often the top jobs of industry, the top jobs of business, and the professions, and even the academic world are closed against the really capable and talented woman.
>
> We can open, and we are opening, the doors of public service and I think this is going to influence some other sectors as well. My whole aim in promoting women and picking out more women to serve in this administration is to underline our profound belief that we can waste no talent, we can frustrate no creative power, we can neglect no skill in our search for an open and just challenging society. There is no place for discrimination of any kind in American life. There must be places for citizens who can think and create and act.[53]

Appointments continued to be made. In October, at his last press conference before the election, Johnson announced that over 1600 women had been appointed or promoted to grades GS 12 and above.[54] Among the major ones were two ambassadors, an Assistant Secretary of Agriculture, and the first women to serve as members of the Atomic Energy Commission, the Interstate Commerce Commission, and the Board of Directors of the Import-Export Bank.

When he began his campaign to put more women in government, Johnson had promised, "This is no sporadic election year gimmick."[55] A more accurate statement would have been that it was *more* than an election year gimmick. Appointments of women to high positions continued throughout his administration, with some of the most important ones, particularly in the judiciary, coming in the later years of Johnson's term. (See Appendix A for a list of Johnson's female appointments.) But the "upgrading of women in American life" did not become a major goal of his administration. After the 1964 election, the White House no longer received reports on the numbers of women hired or promoted in the executive branch. While assuring department and agency heads of his continuing interest, the President asked that they report their progress to the Chairman of the ICSW, Secretary of Labor Willard Wirtz. Johnson no longer mentioned the subject at his press conferences, and declined Shelton's request for a follow-up interview.[56]

Johnson did not lose his interest in women's advancement; he simply de-emphasized it as he became engrossed in more compelling matters. The War on Poverty and the Great Society legislation became his means of distinguishing himself from Kennedy, and these programs held greater political appeal than the issue of women in government. It is no coincidence that his speeches on women became less frequent around the time these grand strategies began to unfold.[57]

By the late spring of 1964, moreover, Johnson had exploited his women in government campaign to its fullest political potential. It never became a major news story because so few people considered the issue involved to be important. Reporters asked no questions about it at news conferences; it was mentioned only when Johnson brought the matter up himself. The wire services dutifully passed along reports of appointments, but the most serious coverage of the story was written by women of the press whose articles generally appeared in the less important women's sections of newspapers.

Press women, sensing the connection between their own lack of professional stature and the small numbers of newsworthy female politicians, were particularly pleased with Johnson's emphasis on women. Bonnie Angelo, Marguerite Higgins, and Frances Lewine, among others, wrote words of praise for Johnson.[58] Betty Beale reported that Johnson was discouraging visiting dignitaries from appearing before the all-male National Press Club and asserted that this effort, along with his appointments, had made Johnson "the champion of American women."[59]

An article by Marguerite Higgins and Peter Lisagor in the *Saturday Evening Post* praised the President's efforts, but the major weekly news magazines—*Time, Newsweek, U.S. News and World Report*—carried only brief accounts. *Newsweek* pegged its story on the President's failure to reach his goal within thirty days, and ridiculed his inept handling of announcements.[60]

The campaign to put women in government did win political friends for Johnson. After the setbacks of the Kennedy years, party women were particularly delighted. Campaign workers such as India Edwards believed Johnson's stance would attract female votes. Esther Peterson, who began plans to organize women for Johnson immediately after Kennedy's death, was also gratified at Johnson's interest.[61] While she did not share other party women's enthusiasm for presidential appointments, she happily supported presidential appeals to the executive branch. Johnson's positive statements assured the PCSW's successors of presidential backing, increasing both their stature and their expectations that progress could occur. Johnson gave a tremendous boost to Peterson's strategy of building public recognition of women's problems. Following the meetings of January 17, she sent him a note of generous praise: "You did more for American women Friday than has been done in a generation."[62]

Johnson's pronouncements also generated enthusiastic support from organized women's groups. National officers, local chapters and individual members of the Business and Professional Women, the American Association of University Women, the Young Women's Christian Association, Zonta International, and the Lucy Stone League sent telegrams and letters of support to the President. Many correspondents also sent names of possible appointees.[63] The BPW launched a nationwide talent search to help the President locate qualified women, and offered to make its list available to businesses, industries, and professional groups seeking highly skilled women to employ.[64] At its annual convention that summer, the BPW presented a special award to Johnson "recognizing his contribution to accelerating the progress of women." Esther Peterson, who accepted the award for Johnson, was particularly pleased to have the support of this "largely Republican" group.[65] The American Federation of Government Employees also sent Johnson a resolution of commendation.[66]

Aside from comments that the issue was too trivial to merit presidential attention, there was no objection to Johnson's efforts to place more women in government. All the mail received by the White House on the subject was favorable, and, to the extent that women were organized to do so, they responded positively.[67] Yet no great outpouring of public sentiment indicated to Johnson that he needed to move further in his pledge to make the upgrading of women a "major goal" of his administration. He had already done more than the public expected; even from organized women, there was no pressure for further action.

By the summer of 1964, moreover, Johnson's political situation was dramatically improved. He had established his own distinct identity as a strong champion of civil rights, and as the commander in chief of the War on Poverty. He had pulled the country through the crisis of Kennedy's assassination, demonstrated that he was a capable leader, and was assured of an easy nomination by his party. When the Republicans nominated conservative Barry Goldwater as their presidential candidate in July, Johnson confidently shifted his focus from victory to landslide. There was no need to undertake further efforts on behalf of women; any further initiatives would need to come from women themselves.

Johnson's brief woman-in-government campaign affected policy development in three ways. Least significant, although worthy of note, was its impact on federal employment policy. Johnson forced the executive branch to notice the distribution of women in the upper levels of the civil service, as well as in appointive positions. Following upon Kennedy's 1962 directive limiting the sex preference specifications for hiring, Johnson's efforts moved the government another small step closer to the PCSW's ideal, a "showcase" of equal employment opportunity for women. The Civil Service Commission did little beyond issuing platitudinous statements on the issue until 1967, when an executive order mandated more serious measures, but Kennedy's and Johnson's statements alerted government personnel officers to begin thinking in terms of a new responsibility.[68]

Wishing to win favor with the new President, several administrators made genuine and successful efforts to seek out more women employees. Since records were not kept in a form allowing year-to-year comparison until 1967, one can only estimate the impact of Johnson's efforts; it appears that at least while reports went directly to the White House, women made some astonishingly rapid gains in GS grades 12–16. Isabelle Shelton, recalling "those few months," said, "There's never been anything like it— before or since."[69]

A second area of significance concerns the implications of Johnson's activities for the bodies charged with continuing the PCSW's work. Johnson's firm statements in support of upgrading women's status energized both the Interdepartmental Committee and the Citizens' Advisory Council on the Status of Women. Even though Johnson's actions fell short of his promises, his words signalled these groups to proceed, and gave them a sense of the importance of their work.

But the chief significance of Johnson's women-in-government campaign is that it raised the policy discussion of equal employment opportunity for women to a new level. Perhaps the greatest power given to a respected president is the power to bless—to use the "bully pulpit" to draw public attention to an issue, and make it politically significant. In 1964, Johnson had that power. He employed it most effectively in furthering the cause of civil rights; his attempt to bless women's employment issues was not successful in an immediate political sense, chiefly because women were not prepared to respond as a political group. Yet by focusing on women's employment issues more intensely than any of his predecessors, and by giving the idea of women's advancement his unqualified support, Johnson encouraged a small but important group of women to go forward with a process that would eventually politicize women's issues.

The strategy and timing of Johnson's campaign deserve brief consideration. Looking for a way to get more women into the government, Johnson borrowed from the system he helped develop for the President's Committee on Equal Employment Opportunity, which he headed as Kennedy's Vice President. Just as the PCEEO used employment goals and periodic reports to increase employment opportunities for blacks in private industry, Johnson used these tactics to improve opportunities for women in the executive branch of the government. His actions suggested a connection between efforts to eliminate employment discrimination based on sex and that based on race. On February 8, 1964, this connection emerged in a potent new form. Johnson's efforts to employ more women in government were just getting underway as the House of Representatives began to debate the employment provisions of the Civil Rights Bill.

4

Linking Sex and Race, 1964

In 1964, after forty years of stalemate, women's political issues appeared to be moving into a new and more positive era. A conscious federal policy on women was taking shape, based on an acceptance of the fact that women's contributions to society were not limited to the homemaking role, and a realization that women were stymied from making their maximum potential contribution. Reflecting the tenet of the Kennedy and Johnson administrations that an active federal government could facilitate development of a better society, this policy held that government could play a role in ameliorating women's situation, to the benefit of individual women and society as a whole. A general outlook rather than a call to specific action, this developing policy aroused minimal political interest: it was neither widely acclaimed nor opposed.

Public indifference remained the greatest hurdle to specific action, but there were other obstacles as well, centering around the old debate between supporters of women's protective legislation and proponents of an Equal Rights Amendment. The President's Commission on the Status of Women (PCSW) managed to downplay this split, but had not fully resolved it; there was still no general agreement on what was meant by equality for women. Early in 1964, in a brief, unexpected, and crucial showdown, the old division of opinion focused on the matter of equal employment opportunity for women.

Regardless of differing views on protective laws and the ERA, everyone concerned with women's situation could agree that job discrimination was a serious problem. Sex segregation seemed to be built into the job market; the ever-increasing numbers of women moving into the labor force were employed almost exclusively in low paying, low status "women's jobs." This situation was not new, of course, and while a handful of people had long viewed the inequality with dismay, it was just beginning to be discovered as a public problem. The work of the PCSW nurtured the idea that political remedies might be sought for what had generally been viewed as private problems, and fostering public awareness of the arbitrary restrictions on women's employment was one of the Commission's major concerns. The Equal Pay Act, guaranteeing equal pay for equal work, highlighted the fact that there were relatively few instances in which the sexes performed equal work. Explaining the problem, which is generally what the PCSW did, was not nearly so difficult as devising remedies.

One possible solution to employment discrimination lay in following the Fair Employment Practices (FEP) approach designed to alleviate racial discrimination. This method was first used during World War II when black leaders secured an executive order establishing a Fair Employment Practices Committee (FEPC) by threatening President Roosevelt with a massive march on Washington. Roosevelt's FEPC was charged with implementing a policy of nondiscrimination in hiring by the federal government and by private employers operating under government contracts. Discrimination was forbidden on the bases of race, creed, color, or national origin. Lacking enforcement powers, the FEPC had to rely on voluntary cooperation from employers and the pressure of public opinion to implement its decisions.[1]

Each President after Roosevelt set up committees to foster nondiscrimination in federal contracts; Kennedy's PCEEO (President's Committee on Equal Employment Opportunity), chaired by Vice President Johnson, was the strongest of these, for in addition to having some enforcement authority, it also required government contractors to undertake "affirmative action" to insure that discrimination did not occur. But the PCEEO's authority, like that of its predecessors, rested solely on an executive order, and securing appropriations from a hostile Congress was a constant source of worry, as well as a drain on whatever stature and power the Committee was able to establish.[2]

Bills to create a statutory FEPC were introduced in every session of Congress from 1943 to 1963. One, the McConnell bill, passed the House of Representatives in 1951, but Congressional opposition, especially from Southern Democrats, who by virtue of their greater seniority held a disproportionate share of powerful positions, kept most of the bills locked in committee. FEP advocates enjoyed somewhat more success in the states; twenty-eight passed FEP legislation during the postwar years. A few of these laws, like New York's, were effectively enforced, but many were merely statements of good intentions. Spurred on by these limited successes, and at the same time exasperated with the slow pace of improvement, black leaders were, by the early 1960s, increasing their pressure for a federal, statutory FEPC, covering all employment, not just that under federal contract.[3]

As demands for federal action grew, the National Woman's Party and the National Federation of Business and Professional Women's Clubs began to urge that sex be included in each executive order and legislative action banning discrimination based on race, creed, color, and national origin.

While these groups continued to push their Equal Rights Amendment to the Constitution as the ultimate solution to all types of sex discrimination, they believed that adding sex to the standard FEP categories was a logical way to combat employment discrimination against women.

The PCSW agreed in principle that the FEP approach could be helpful, but purposely refrained from advocating mandatory compliance machinery (even for the government contract work in which federal authority was firmly established) apparently in the belief that compliance would not be enforceable.[4] The Commission also specifically rejected a proposal that sex be added to the executive order governing the PCEEO, explaining that sex discrimination involved "problems sufficiently different" from race discrimination "to make separate treatment preferable."[5] The obvious difference was state labor legislation giving women "favored" status, which might be threatened by an outright ban on sex discrimination. A less obvious reason for the Commission's reluctance to link race and sex was the tacit assumption that race discrimination was an intensely more serious problem than sex discrimination. Civil rights was the burning political issue of the early 1960s, and it seemed unthinkable that women should undermine whatever chance blacks had of obtaining an FEP law by adding the burden of an issue with no widespread political support.[6]

Having ruled out coercion of employers, the PCSW hoped to enlighten them; it recommended further studies to combat the commonly held myth that women were unreliable employees. It also sought to ease and improve women's participation in the work force by advocating better counselling services, more training programs, and expanded childcare services. This program of education and exhortation was a painfully slow method of attacking job discrimination, but it was consonant with the PCSW's pragmatic desire to ground its recommendations in the realm of political possibility. Given the apparent lack of public interest in the problem of employment opportunities for women, its conservative suggestions seemed a good way to begin. Perhaps at some future time—when protective legislation applied to all workers, and blacks had secured basic antidiscriminatory legislation—women might press for a statutory ban on sex discrimination in federal contracts and possibly even in private employment.

Yet in July, 1964, just nine months after PCSW's cautious final report, President Johnson signed a bill outlawing sex discrimination in private employment. Esther Peterson called the legislation a "sudden jump through many stages of history."[7] Sex was added to the FEP section of the Civil Rights Act of 1964 by an amendment offered from the House floor. The sex provision was approved without the customary hearings, with only the barest discussion of its implications and with neither widespread support nor opposition. Its passage was secured by an unlikely alliance of Southern

Democratic opponents of the civil rights bill and a small band of feminist lobbyists and Congresswomen.

The unusual circumstances surrounding the amendment's adoption led to accusations that the sex clause was a "fluke," passed without clear intent.[8] The charge contains an element of truth. The impromptu manner in which the amendment was passed forms a marked contrast to the tedious and painful process followed by civil rights groups to win equal employment opportunity legislation for blacks.

But "unusual" political action was *not* so unusual a means of determining public policy towards women. Viewed in the terms of a pluralistic political model, in which various pressure groups bring their forces to bear on the making of public policy, women were not a political group. No grass roots movements pushed for political action on women's behalf; no leaders could claim to represent, or even define, women's interests. Policy decisions affecting women, if they were made in any conscious sense, were not subject to the forces governing most policy matters, and could be made by small numbers of people operating in relative political calm, arguing the merits of their case to those in power.

The major shift in woman's policy during the Kennedy years, for example, can be largely attributed to the efforts of one woman, Esther Peterson, whose authority stemmed more from Kennedy's confidence in her than from any following of her own. And when Anna Rosenberg Hoffman persuaded President Johnson to appoint more women to high level government positions, she relied not on political force, but rather on her long friendship with Johnson, her knowledge of the political situation he faced, and the merits of her argument. When the addition of sex to the Civil Rights Act is viewed as an instance of this same manner of making policy, it becomes somewhat more understandable, although its status as a highly unusual legislative action remains.

The Civil Rights Act of 1964, unlike the sex provision that was added to it, was a classic and highly dramatic example of pressure group politics at work. In the years following *Brown* v. *Board of Education*, the 1954 Supreme Court decision overturning the "separate but equal" justification for racial school segregation, civil rights groups became increasingly active in their efforts to end segregation in schools, restaurants, theatres, buses, and other public places. These groups also sought legislative guarantees for voting rights and equal employment opportunity. The tactic of nonviolent protest, particularly the "sit-in," proved effective in attracting attention, and ultimately, sympathy and support.

The support grew slowly. In 1957, and again in 1960, Congress approved civil rights legislation, but the acts were weak, as they had to be to pass, and satisfied no one. Both presidential candidates in 1960 expressed support for protecting Negroes' rights, although neither promised further legislation. Kennedy advocated the use of executive orders to advance the cause; his government contracts committee, the PCEEO, was a step in that direction. His thin victory over Nixon, and an increasingly difficult relationship with Congress kept a severe check on Kennedy's prestige and authority, making him reluctant to propose legislative action on so controversial a subject as civil rights.

But by the spring of 1963, demand for federal civil rights legislation became too intense and too widespread for Kennedy to ignore. Thanks to recently developed camera technology allowing "on-the-spot" television coverage, a series of clashes between nonviolent civil rights demonstrators and contrastingly brutal police enforcing the laws of segregation were seen in millions of American homes. The protracted demonstration in Birmingham, Alabama in April was particularly significant. Americans watched in horror as police used fire hoses and dogs to break up a peacefully demonstrating crowd of men, women, and children. The civil rights movement had at last captured the public conscience, and Kennedy was forced to send some sort of legislation to Congress.

Anticipating the struggle ahead, the administration drafted a bill meeting the strongest, best-supported demands, and nothing more. Its proposal, sent to Congress in June, banned segregation in places of public accommodation and entertainment, eased restrictions on voting, enabled the Attorney General to file suits to speed school desegregation, and provided for termination of funds to any federally assisted program engaging in discriminatory practices. The bill provided statutory authority for the PCEEO, then operating under executive order, but it pointedly excluded the sort of FEP provisions for which black leaders were asking. Although Kennedy had previously expressed his support for FEP legislation, he feared its inclusion in his civil rights bill would make passage impossible.[9] If the bill failed to pass Congress, the civil rights cause might lose its dearly won momentum, and Kennedy's already shaky leadership ability would be thoroughly undermined.

The House Judiciary Committee, which held extensive hearings on the bill, did not share Kennedy's caution. Under the leadership of Emanuel Celler (D., N.Y.), a subcommittee rewrote the bill, adding an FEP provision to the equal employment opportunity section, Title VII. The new Title would create an Equal Employment Opportunity Commission with broad powers to investigate charges of employment discrimination and to issue judicially enforceable orders.

Alarmed that this addition might jeopardize the entire bill, Kennedy urged House leaders to soften it. During October a compromise bill was worked out, maintaining the employment commission but restricting its powers to investigative and conciliatory functions; it could compel enforcement only by bringing suits in federal courts.[10] The compromise bill, with Kennedy's backing and the support of House leaders of both parties, cleared the Judiciary Committee, and was sent to the House Rules Committee on November 21, the day before Kennedy's assassination.

Now the fate of the bill was in the hands of "Judge" Howard Smith (D., Va.), chairman of the Rules Committee, and one of the most intransigent defenders of states' rights and segregation. A majority of the Rules Committee members favored the bill, but the chairman had the power to hold it until he wished to introduce it, and Smith was in no hurry.

At a special joint session of Congress on November 27, President Johnson made clear his intention to secure the bill's passage. "No memorial oration or eulogy," he said, "could more eloquently honor President Kennedy's memory than the earliest possible passage of the civil rights bill for which he fought so long."[11] Johnson designated the bill as a top legislative priority.

Public sentiment for civil rights legislation grew during the national mourning for Kennedy, and Johnson's maneuvering increased the pressure on Judge Smith to bring the bill before his committee. Threatened with a discharge petition that would remove the bill from any control he might exert, Smith finally agreed to hold committee hearings in return for a promise that no attempt would be made to cut off debate on amendments once the bill reached the House floor.[12] The hearings began in January, 1964.

As it became increasingly apparent that the bill would pass the House, Southern Democrats began to search for amendments to weaken it. Administration forces, carefully marshalling their support with help from the White House, resolved to accept no amendments. Generally, they had the votes to make this position stick.

The National Woman's Party, perennial champion of the ERA, followed the bill's fortunes with great interest. In December, while Smith still held the bill from the Rules Committee, the NWP's National Council resolved, in accordance with its established policy, to seek an amendment adding sex to the prohibited bases of discrimination.[13]

Smith expressed an interest in the NWP's request. He first mentioned the subject early in the Rules Committee hearings when questioning Emanuel Celler, who was testifying as Chairman of the Judiciary Committee and floor leader of the bill. Smith wondered why sex had not been included along with race in the bill.

> Mr. Celler: This is a civil rights bill.
> The Chairman [Smith]: Don't women have civil rights?
> Mr. Celler: They have lots of them. They are supermen.

....

The Chairman: I have not found out yet why you did not put "sex" in.

Mr. Celler: Do you want to put it in, Mr. Chairman?

The Chairman: I think I will offer an amendment. The National Women's Party were serious about it.[14]

Sex discrimination was mentioned briefly several more times by Southerners on the Committee. Katharine St. George (R., N.Y.), a committee member who favored the bill, also voiced some interest in the issue, complaining several times that women suffered from discrimination.[15]

The subject was raised again, on January 26, when Smith appeared on the nationally broadcast television show, "Meet the Press." White House correspondent May Craig, known and frequently ridiculed for her interest in women's issues, asked Smith if he intended to introduce an amendment to Title VII guaranteeing women equal rights. Smith indicated that he might do so.[16]

Such action would not be unprecedented. A sex clause had been included in the only FEP bill ever to pass either house of Congress, the McConnell bill, which passed the House of Representatives after an all-night debate in 1951. An amendment from the floor added sex, physical disability, and political affiliation to race, creed, and color as bases upon which discrimination was to be prohibited. But by 1964, the political stakes involved in civil rights legislation had increased dramatically, and because the bipartisan coalition supporting the bill appeared to hold a strong majority, it was unlikely to accept any amendment perceived as weakening. Since a sex provision would dilute the time, money and effort that the proposed FEPC would otherwise spend on race problems, the NWP's amendment did not seem to have much chance of success.

Still, the idea appealed to the bill's opponents for a number of reasons. Sex discrimination was becoming a fashionable topic in Washington, thanks to the President's efforts to place more women in top level government jobs.[17] A radical proposal for ending sex discrimination, coming from conservative, segregationist Southerners would be potentially embarrassing to the President, especially if he had to denounce it to save the civil rights bill.

House members, too, might be hesitant to cast an "antiwoman" vote. Since the amendment was not overtly racist, it might draw support from some of the bill's proponents. St. George expressed an interest during the Rules Committee hearings; perhaps others would join her.

More important than these considerations was the fact that Southern Democrats could use the sex issue to demonstrate the absurdity and futility of federal legislation in the matter of race relations. Believing that public furor over the race issue made it hard for Representatives to remain objective, Smith and his cohorts felt they could not argue directly on the matter of race. They could, however, ridicule the bill's radical philosophy indirectly. Women, like racial minorities, were discriminated against, but the reasons for sex discrimination were generally acceptable and did not excite such emotional fervor. An amendment seeking the same rights for women as the bill provided for racial minorities would be subject to derision, and would help Smith make his point; it would simply be carrying a ridiculous argument to its extreme.

While proposing the amendment with tongue in cheek, Smith could adopt a chivalrous pose that was entirely consistent with the Southern tradition he claimed to be defending. Southern Democrats had in the past harbored a sympathetic outlook toward (if not a genuine commitment to) the Equal Rights Amendment. Much of Southern industry, notably textile manufacture, depended on cheap female labor, and strong protective legislation for women threatened the economic setup. Because Southern employers believed, along with the Women's Bureau, that the ERA would outlaw protective laws, they looked favorably on it, and their representatives in Congress were not averse to blending the arguments of feminism and chivalry in support of an antilabor position. Thus, pedestal-ensconced white women were said to need protection from Negroes, but not from sweatshop conditions. Smith's presentation of a sex amendment, both mocking and chivalrous, would be precisely in line with this time-honored stance.[18]

These explanations for Smith's proposal of a sex amendment are, of necessity, conjecture. To his dying day, Smith never admitted to being anything but "serious" about the amendment.[19]

Meanwhile, Martha Griffiths (D., Mich.) was independently preparing to introduce a sex amendment to Title VII. Griffiths, who was sufficiently respected by her colleagues to have been elected to the prestigious Committee on Ways and Means, harbored a decidedly feminist outlook. Unlike the Southerners and liberals who believed a sex clause would weaken Title VII, Griffiths concluded that the addition of sex would actually strengthen it. Title VII was designed to insure that persons were hired solely on the basis of their abilities; because sex discrimination was so pervasive, it had to be prohibited along with the other types of discrimination for the merit principle to work.

Griffiths supported the civil rights bill, and believed its passage was inevitable. Along with both its advocates and detractors, she felt it would become a legislative landmark. Women were excluded the last time such an important decision was made: neither the Reconstruction Amendments, nor their later interpretation by the courts extended to women the privileges and protections granted to the freedmen. This time Griffiths intended to see that women were not overlooked.

Garnering votes for her amendment would be difficult. She expected opposition from Celler, in whose Judiciary Committee the ERA was customarily laid to rest, and from other liberals who would see the amendment as merely another controversy to bog down the bill. Learning that Smith was planning to introduce an amendment similar to hers, she decided to let him offer it, for his sponsorship would guarantee the votes of approximately one hundred Southern Democrats she felt unable to secure on her own.[20]

The bill, which moved from the Rules Committee to the House floor on January 31, was the subject of several questions at the President's news conference the following day. Johnson reiterated his hope that the measure would pass without "any crippling amendments."[21] A reporter asked if he would support an amendment including women in the civil rights bill, noting that the Democratic platform of 1960 expressed support for "legislation which will guarantee to women equality of rights under the law." (This was the ERA plank which had so troubled Esther Peterson; see Chapter 2.) Johnson replied:

> I supported that platform and embraced that platform, and stated that view in 43 States in the Union. I realize there has been discrimination in the employment of women, and I am doing my best to do something about it. I am hopeful that in the next month we will have made substantial advances in that field.[22]

This skillful evasion showed the President's interest in alleviating employment discrimination, but seemed to suggest that putting more women in government would take care of the problem. Yet Johnson did not rule out support for a sex amendment. In all likelihood, his personal opinion was one of indifference. His main concern was that the House would pass a civil rights bill which the public would perceive as strong, and which would also be able to garner enough support to override a Senate filibuster. That goal in itself was sufficiently difficult to achieve without worrying about the women; they would have to take care of themselves.

Back on the House floor, Smith and his forces were using the time secured by their agreement to make numerous speeches and to propose a long list of amendments. Between January 31 and February 10, 122 amendments were offered; all but 28 were rejected.[23] John Dowdy (D., Tex.), who worked closely with Smith, introduced amendments adding sex to Titles II, III, IV, and V of the bill, but each was handily defeated. The only debate on any of these amendments arose over the one to Title II, the public accommodations section, when the desirability of sex-segregated restrooms was briefly discussed.[24]

Title VII, as May Craig suggested, was the logical place for a sex amendment, and on February 8, as the House began consideration of the equal employment opportunity section, Smith introduced it himself. Since no committee had considered the amendment, and the Senate did not later discuss it in any detail, the two hour debate that followed comprised practically the entire legislative history of the sex provision.[25] The debate reflected the volatile nature of its topics—race and sex—and provided little guidance to those who would eventually have to interpret Congressional intent. It contained a dose of levity, some conflicting speculation about the amendment's effects, and strong overtones of the continuing debate over the Equal Rights Amendment.

Smith claimed to be "very serious" about his amendment, and argued that it would redress some of the real grievances women suffered in the workplace.[26] But his introductory remarks barely mentioned this subject, and dwelt instead on ridiculing the idea of "rights." He read a constituent's letter contending that since females in the population greatly outnumbered males, many women were being deprived of their "right to a husband." Exclaiming that Congress should attend to this "grave injustice . . . particularly in an election year," Smith was several times interrupted by laughter.[27]

Celler continued the joking as he rose in opposition to the amendment. He explained his secret for marital harmony: ". . . I usually have the last two words, and those words are 'Yes, dear.'" At one point he was even moved to poetry:

Lives there a man with hide so tough
Who says, "Two sexes are not enough."

In a more serious vein, Celler denounced the amendment as an "entering wedge" for the ERA, and recited the standard catalogue of difficulties attendant upon legal equality of the sexes. He argued further that women, unlike Negroes, were making "real and genuine progress" since the passage of the Equal Pay Act the year before.

The keystone of Celler's argument was a letter from the Department of Labor, explaining Women's Bureau opposition to the amendment. The letter quoted Esther Peterson who reasoned that since the PCSW had decided sex discrimination should be attacked separately from other types, an amendment adding sex to the civil rights bill "would not be in the best interests of women at this time."

Peterson did not write the letter Celler presented, for she had been out of Washington at the time, but she did agree with the Department's position, principally from fear that a sex amendment would jeopardize the bill.[28] The fact that the letter was signed not by Peterson, but by a man, led one Southern gentleman to remark in mock feministic dismay,

... the letter from the Women's Bureau ... opposing this equal rights for women amendment was signed by a man. I think there is no need for me to say more. Even the Department set up by the U.S. Government for the benefit of women is opposed to equal rights in employment for women.[29]

Women in the House must have felt this dismay more seriously, for they did not generally share Peterson's fear that the sex amendment would hurt the civil rights bill. Nor did they, as a group, subscribe to the WB's labor oriented outlook towards protective legislation and the ERA; of the ten women in the House at the time, half had sponsored the ERA.[30] Six women participated in the debate on the sex amendment; there is no record of the position, if any, taken by the other four, although Frieda Gehlen, who has studied women members of Congress, asserts that they voted for the amendment.[31] Of the six who spoke, only Edith Green (D., Ore.) argued against the amendment; the other five urged its adoption.

Martha Griffiths made the strongest appeal. She began by objecting to the tone of the debate, stating ". . . if there had been any necessity to have pointed out that women were a second-class sex, the laughter would have proved it,"—and went on to argue that the bill would make white women "last at the hiring gate." Employers would fear prosecution if they refused to hire qualified black men and women, but white women would have no protection at all under the law.

Griffiths emphasized the effects on white women, but her testimony also reflected the uncertain status of black women under the bill's provisions. She argued first that because of the bill, black women would have "open entree" into fields previously reserved for white males. Later she suggested the contradictory possibility that black women would not be able to secure jobs reserved for men only as long as sex discrimination remained legal.

Either of these conflicting outcomes was possible under Title VII. With or without Smith's amendment, the law's enforcers would have to deal with the question of sex discrimination: to decide, as in the examples Griffiths mentioned, whether a company with an all-white, all-male labor force was guilty of race discrimination for refusing to hire a black female. The bill's drafters had apparently overlooked this fact, or deemed it inconsequential. The unspoken premise of the equal employment opportunity provision was that it would place black males on a more equal footing *vis à vis* white males. This male bias, which grew naturally out of a social attitude that idealized men's role as breadwinner and women's as homemaker, was the main target of Griffith's attack.

Representatives Frances Bolton (R., Ohio), Katharine St. George (R., N.Y.), Edna F. Kelly (D., N.Y.), and Catherine May (R., Wash.) joined Griffiths in urging the amendment's passage. All denounced discrimination against women, and several made reference to the ERA, evidencing a level of interest which would seem to justify Peterson's fears that the Constitutional amendment was not a dead issue. Catherine May lamented the lack of progress on the ERA, and supported the sex amendment on behalf of the women's organizations who viewed it "as the one possibility we may have of getting effective action."

Several women offered opinions on the crucial issue of the amendment's effects on state labor laws applying only to women. Griffiths contended that such laws protected "men's rights to better paying jobs," and argued that Title VII, even without the sex amendment, would jeopardize protective legislation; under its provisions black women would surely challenge these laws, with a fair chance of success. If organized labor wished to maintain protective legislation, Griffiths said, it would

> . . . do far better to support this amendment and ask for a savings clause in this law and we will all start even in the morning.

But no clause exempting protective laws from the bill's coverage was proposed.

Katharine St. George delivered a fiery invective against protective laws, stating that women neither needed nor wanted "special privileges," but only "this little crumb of equality." Her testimony suggested that the sex amendment would invalidate laws applying only to women.

Edna F. Kelly appears to have misunderstood St. George's meaning, and referred to her assurances that the sex amendment would not destroy protective laws. Urging support for the amendment, Kelly stated, "I believe in equality for women and am sure the acceptance of the amendment will not repeal the protective laws of the several States."

This collective testimony fell woefully short of clarifying Congressional intent regarding protective legislation, but it did, at least, pertain to the subject. For the ten Southern males who, along with Smith, voiced support for the amendment, the statement of J. Russell Tuten (D., Ga.) will serve as an example.

> Some men in some areas of the country might support legislation which would discriminate against women, but never let it be said that a southern gentleman would vote for such legislation.

With one exception, all the men who spoke in favor of the amendment later voted against the bill. That exception was Ross Bass (D., Tenn.). His testimony was as exceptional as his vote, for it raised one of the few specific issues of the debate. Bass pointed out the problems of airline stewardesses who were forced to leave their jobs once they married. The plight of stewardesses, under the new, nonsexist term, "flight cabin attendants," would be one of the early major issues brought to the Equal Employment Opportunity Commission.

Edith Green presented the only female opposition to the amendment, but her credentials as a supporter of women's rights made her a formidable opponent. Green was a driving force behind the Equal Pay Act of 1963 and had also served as a member of the PCSW. Her past actions spoke eloquently of her desire to end sex discrimination, but she did not believe this was "the time or place for this amendment." Green deplored the fact that the amendment had not been studied by any committee, pointing out that biological differences between men and women would create problems for employers which should have been carefully discussed. She reminded the House that the bill's main purpose was to end discrimination against Negroes, and warned that the sex amendment would

> clutter up the bill and it may later . . . be used to help destroy this section . . . by some of the very people who today support it.

While she might be called "an Uncle Tom—or perhaps an Aunt Jane," Green expressed a willingness to wait for an end to sex discrimination if waiting would help solve the greater and more serious problem of race discrimination.

Toward the end of the debate, several liberal Congressmen joined Green and Celler in denouncing the amendment. Attempting to defend PCSW policy, James Roosevelt (D., Calif.) read into the *Record* the impressive list of Commission members, and invoked his mother's memory in behalf of the "responsible" position. But when the vote came, the House accepted the amendment, 168–133.

The vote was decisive, and surely a surprise to all parties. Since the decision was made by a teller vote, it is impossible to pinpoint the sources of the amendment's support, or to speculate with much accuracy on the reasons for its success.[32] Surely the bulk of the 168 favorable votes came from the bloc of Southern Democrats and other opponents of the bill, but this group was not large enough to pass the amendment without help. Only 130 Representatives voted against the bill in the final roll call, and it is unlikely that all of these were present to vote on the sex amendment. Adding to this overestimation the five women who voted both for the bill and the amendment, still leaves 33 votes unexplained. If one assumes that the proportion of the bill's opponents and proponents voting on the sex amendment was the same as their proportion on the final roll call, 71 "unexplained" votes result. By any calculation, a sizeable part of the amendment's support had to come from males who eventually voted for the bill; according to our two rough estimations, the figures are 20 percent and 42 percent, respectively.[33]

This undetermined yet significant number of Representatives who broke from Celler's leadership is termed the "unexplained" vote for good reason. An unrecorded teller vote allowed legislators the opportunity to weaken a measure which they felt compelled to support "on the record."[34] This tactic may have been employed by Representatives who felt the sex amendment would weaken the proposed employment commission. Alternatively, the unexplained votes may be accepted at face value as positive approval for sex's inclusion.

The NWP claimed credit for the victory, citing as evidence its extensive lobbying campaign.[35] While the NWP deserves credit for instigating the amendment, its lobby was more notable for its persistence than its success, and its claim for full responsibility is dubious. There is no accurate gauge of NWP support in the House since the main object of its lobbying, the ERA, had for so long been bottled up in committee. A crude indication might be drawn from the fact that a quarter of the Representatives in the 88th Congress had listed their names as sponsors of the ERA.[36] Not all of these were necessarily die-hard supporters of women's rights; antilabor views doubtlessly influenced some of the sponsors. Sponsorship, moreover, was relatively meaningless as long as the Judiciary Committee held the bill.

Martha Griffiths dismissed the importance of the NWP, and contended that the arguments she presented on the House floor were responsible for the amendment's passage.[37] She was in a good position to know where the support came from; as one of the tellers who counted the votes, she saw who voted for the amendment. Her explanation is self-serving, but makes sense when tempered with the consideration that the subject of discrimination against working women was not new to the House. Years of unproductive debate over the ERA and repeated hearings and debate on the Equal Pay bill had at least familiarized legislators with the topic. Just eight months earlier, the first session of this same Congress approved the Equal Pay Act. The sex amendment was a dramatic step beyond equal pay, but the civil rights bill itself was a dramatic extension of federal authority, and Griffiths provided a compelling justification for including women in that extension. Applying the same argument used against racial discrimination, Griffiths insisted that merit was the only proper criterion for employment decisions. If Congress accepted this argument for blacks, it was hard to refute its application to women. Since there were no powerful political blocs of women to deal with (the PCSW obviously did not qualify), Congress was free to legislate on the basis of Griffiths' argument. It seems fair to postulate that Griffiths secured at least a large portion of the unexplained votes.

Yet as Edith Green accused, the sex provision being considered in isolation "would not receive 100 votes."[38] It was Southern support that carried the amendment, and that support was conditioned upon opposition to the civil rights bill. Even though it won House approval, the sex provision was suspect. It would later be said to have been "conceived out of wedlock."[39] A New York *Herald Tribune* editorial called the amendment "an unplanned by-product of a confused debate."[40]

The lack of planning became evident at the House's next meeting on Monday, February 10, the day scheduled for a final vote on the bill.[41] Since Smith's hastily drawn amendment failed to include sex in all relevant sections of Title VII, Frances Bolton offered a further amendment to correct his mistakes. Neither Smith's nor Bolton's amendment added sex to the section exempting from the bill's coverage certain jobs having religion and national origin as a *"bona fide* occupational qualification." The *bfoq* exception was intended to allow, for example, a French restaurant to advertise for and hire a French cook, or a Catholic school to specify that its teachers be Catholic. Race was not included in the exception. Charles Goodell (R., N.Y.) pointed out that in many instances sex might be a *bfoq*, citing the example of an "elderly woman who wants a female nurse." Bolton agreed to include Goodell's suggestion in her amendment, and the House quickly approved it. The *bfoq* exception merited more discussion than it received, for the strictness of its interpretation would determine the effectiveness of the sex clause. In its rush to move on to the final vote and adjourn for the traditional Lincoln's birthday recess, the House was in no mood to discuss such details.

The House did appear determined to retain the sex provision. It turned down a weakening amendment requiring any person filing charges of sex discrimination to sign an oath stating that his or her spouse, if any, was unemployed.[42] Just before the final roll call, when most members presumably were present, a second vote was called on the sex amendment; once again the House approved it, this time by a voice vote.[43] The House then passed the entire bill, 290–130.[44]

Two days later, the Citizens' Advisory Council on the Status of Women wrestled with the implications of the House vote at its first meeting.[45] The CAC, and its in-government counterpart, the Interdepartmental Committee on the Status of Women, had been established to carry on the work of the PCSW. Composed chiefly of former PCSW members, and supported by Department of Labor funds and staff, the CAC generally subscribed to the philosophy of the woman responsible for its existence, Esther Peterson. Both Peterson and Secretary of Labor Willard Wirtz attended this first CAC meeting. Any action taken by the group would bear a close resemblance to the Department of Labor's wishes.

The Department's initial opposition to a sex amendment had now to be reassessed in the light of the House's action. An endorsement of the amendment, repudiating the PCSW and Department of Labor's position was impossible; the amendment had not been carefully studied, and might yet be used against the civil rights bill. But House approval of a ban of sex discrimination made opposition to such a desirable goal difficult to justify. Even if opposition were not a disservice to the women the CAC was charged with helping, it could be embarrassing, as the jibes thrown at the Women's Bureau during the House debate had shown. If the Senate approved the amendment despite a stand opposing it, the CAC risked losing any claim to authority as a voice for women's interests. Deciding to take no action, "because it was too early to discuss not only the legislative wisdom but also the unexplored policy and administrative difficulties involved," the council was stepping back, however slightly, from the Labor Department's earlier opposition.[46]

At his news conference of February 29, Johnson expressed support for the House bill "exactly in its present form," without specific reference to the sex clause.[47] Throughout March and April he continued the speeches promoting his efforts to end sex discrimination in federal employment, but did not link these efforts to the civil rights bill. He was not forced to make a public commitment on the issue, a fact which testifies to the low level of public interest. If coverage by the news media is any indication, the amendment seems to have been forgotten almost immediately after its passage in the House. But behind the scenes, feminists were at work trying to garner support in the Senate and to goad the President into a more active espousal of the sex provision.

The NWP, of course, continued its lobbying, and Pauli Murray, the lawyer who developed the PCSW's argument against the ERA, wrote a "Memorandum in Support of Retaining the Sex Amendment," which the Business and Professional Women's lobbyists distributed in the Senate.[48] Several women, including members of the Texas Business and Professional Women, sent letters and telegrams to the President requesting his support; they received polite responses from Esther Peterson noting that a sex clause was in the bill.[49]

During early spring, the civil rights bill underwent another rewriting, as proponents attempted to find a formula acceptable to two-thirds of the Senators, the number necessary to end the filibuster. What eventually became the "Dirksen-Mansfield compromise" was formulated in a series of private sessions; there is no way to know why the sex clause remained.[50] Caroline Bird, a journalist who talked to some of the women lobbying for the amendment, says that at one point Senator Dirksen (R., Ill.), whose support was crucial, wanted to drop the sex clause, but was somehow dissuaded.[51] Martha Griffiths credits Senator Margaret Chase Smith (R., Me.) with keeping the clause in the bill.[52]

It is unlikely that Johnson or any of his aides argued for the sex amendment when issues more crucial to them, such as the survival of the employment commission, were at stake. Yet as the compromise began to form, and chances for passage appeared more favorable, Johnson spoke somewhat more freely on the subject. In April he personally answered a letter from the Texas Business and Professional Women saying,

> With respect to the inclusion of sex in Title VII, it is the firm conviction of the Administration that equal opportunity for women. . .should be the governing principle in private industry, and it is the hope of the Administration that the bill will be enacted in its present form.[53]

In May the compromise was secured, and on June 10 the Senate invoked cloture for the first time ever on a civil rights bill. On June 12, Johnson told delegates to a conference celebrating the effective date of the Equal Pay Act:

> The glory and greatness of America lies in. . .the open door of equal opportunity for all our citizens regardless of their sex or their religion or their race.[54]

With the filibuster broken, the bill's safety was assured. House approval of the compromise quickly followed Senate passage, and on July 2, Johnson signed the Civil Rights Act of 1964.

The Senate compromise made drastic changes in Title VII. The Equal Employment Opportunity Commission—the name given the FEPC created by the Title—lost its power to bring suits; the burden of enforcement fell to the individual complainant, with the EEOC serving only as an investigative and mediating agency.[55]

Itself the result of a political dispute only partially resolved during the legislative process, the EEOC inherited the totally unresolved issues involved in the sex clause. Solution of these issues would require application of political pressure, for the EEOC was tailored to pluralistic, pressure group politics; it could be made to work for and by those groups who could muster sufficient political strength. The arguments of a woman in the right place at the right time would not be sufficient to influence the EEOC; enforcement of the sex provision could be achieved only through the power of numbers and organization.

The CAC and ICSW, along with the state Commissions on the Status of Women formed a basis for organization, although their ties to WB's protectionist philosophy and their reluctance to link race and sex discrimination complicated their response to the new law. The next chapter discusses these groups' involvement in the War on Poverty, and explains how the government's response to that involvement began to alter their thinking.

5

The War on Poverty and Feminist Consciousness, 1964-1965

In 1963 the President's Commission on the Status of Women (PCSW) said that sex discrimination was sufficiently different from race discrimination to require a separate remedy. Inclusion of sex in Title VII of the Civil Rights Act of 1964 forced the groups responsible for carrying out the PCSW's work to reevaluate this view. The reevaluation occurred as Johnson's administration embarked on a new crusade to assure equal opportunity, the War on Poverty. Like the Civil Rights Act, the War on Poverty focused on concerns of race rather than gender, but exerted a profound influence on the developing concept of equal opportunity for women.

The War on Poverty had its intellectual origins in a series of economic and sociological studies undertaken in the late 1950s and early 1960s which documented the continued existence of poverty in the midst of American affluence and questioned the theory that general economic growth would eventually eradicate the problem.[1] Drawing attention to poverty's social consequences, the new studies suggested a refinement in the concept of equal opportunity.

Inferior housing, education, and medical care caused physical and psychic scars that were not easily overcome. Along with poor health, an attitude of hopelessness and alienation trapped the poor in a "cycle of poverty" which passed from generation to generation.[2] Deprived of the knowledge, skills, attitudes, and motivation developed by the more fortunate members of society, the poor and their children were denied the opportunity to participate in the system of rewards and incentives upon which the American economy was based. Poverty, in this view, was not merely a result of unequal opportunity, but one of its chief causes.[3]

Perception of poverty as a political issue coincided with the civil rights movement's sudden spurt of political legitimacy during Kennedy's presidency, and the two developments were closely related. Black people, about 10 percent of the population, comprised an unduly large proportion of the poor: one-half of all black families were poor, and one-fifth of all poor families were black. With the Civil Rights Act, the federal government accepted the responsibility for protecting equal employment opportunity; the idea that poverty deprived its victims of equal opportunities indicated a need for further governmental action. The War on Poverty was thus an important refinement in the concept of governmental assurance of equal opportunity.

Beyond its importance to the theory of equal opportunity, the War on Poverty had a special significance for the Status of Women groups. After explaining the setup and membership of these organizations, this chapter will examine how their involvement with the Women's Job Corps aroused the first stirrings of a feminist political consciousness. Strengthened by the threats to women's advancement perceived in the Moynihan Report, this new consciousness shaped the thinking of the Status of Women groups, and prepared them to fight for the enforcement of Title VII's sex provision.

Upon the completion of its work, Kennedy's Commission on the Status of Women recommended the establishment of two federal bodies to oversee the implementation of its recommendations and carry on its work. An Executive Order of November 1, 1963, created in Interdepartmental Committee on the Status of Women (ICSW) composed of cabinet-level officials, and a Citizens' Advisory Council on the Status of Women (CAC) made up of carefully selected private citizens.[4] The CAC operated under the direction of the ICSW, which in turn was responsible to the President. Secretary of Labor Willard Wirtz chaired the ICSW, and Esther Peterson, Assistant Secretary of Labor, Director of the Women's Bureau, and the driving force behind these organizations, served as Vice Chairman.[5] These federal groups were joined by a growing number of state organizations also devoted to improving women's status.

Even before the PCSW finished its work, several states and cities appointed their own Commissions on the Status of Women, and, under Esther Peterson's direction, the Women's Bureau moved to encourage this development. It sponsored a series of regional conferences to disseminate the PCSW's ideas and to stimulate discussion of women's status.[6] Through its five regional offices, the Bureau worked with women's organizations to press for the creation of commissions in each state. By the summer of 1964 when the Civil Rights Act was signed, 32 states had established official groups to study the needs of women and how these were, or might be, affected by governmental actions.[7] Forty-nine states (all but Texas) eventually created such commissions. Typically promulgated by the governor and composed of his appointees, the state commissions provided a means for women to meet and reflect upon their status; for most of the appointees, it was a novel experience. The Women's Bureau was creating a constituency for itself, opening new channels of communication among women, and encouraging the political consideration of women's issues.

The CAC was particularly interested in fostering the work of the state commissions. To facilitate communication among these groups, and to encourage coordination of state and federal efforts in advancing women's status, the CAC asked the ICSW to help sponsor a national conference for the leaders of the state commissions. The first such conference in June 1964 drew 85 people representing 32 states to Washington. Conferees discussed the varied concerns of their commissions: updating state minimum wage laws, investigating educational and day-care services, examining discriminatory inheritance laws. They also considered ways to handle the problem of a "facetious" press, and methods of broadening participation in their work.[8] Attendance at the second national conference, held in July, 1965, rose to 416.[9] An impressive array of dignitaries, including the President and Vice President, addressed the participants, reassuring them of the importance of their work.[10] Interest in the status of women was clearly growing, both in Washington and within the state commissions.

The Status of Women groups existed to advocate change; yet on both the state and federal levels their membership was far from radical. Governors could, and did, use their appointments to state commissions to repay women who had performed traditionally feminine campaign services, such as arranging tea parties for candidates to meet prominent women. But the state commissions also included experts in various fields of women's interests, and recognized leaders of women's civic and professional organizations. Among the more notable chairmen of the state commissions were Anne Firor Scott of North Carolina, who later became known for her work in women's history; Esther Saperstein, a member of the Illinois House of Representatives, who, after serving on the Illinois commission, sought and won a seat in the State Senate; and Kathryn Clarenbach, Director of Continuing Education at the University of Wisconsin, who became the first president of the National Organization for Women.

ICSW members, as stipulated by executive order, were cabinet officials; their loyalty to the President naturally overrode any personal commitments either to change or to the status quo.[11] The ICSW was created to insure that the men who set policy and directed the day-to-day affairs of the executive branch were conscious of the ways in which governmental policy affected women. Since these officials frequently had more pressing concerns, most ICSW members had official deputies who represented departmental interests and kept them advised of the ICSW's work. Several deputies—notably Evelyn Harrison of the Civil Service Commission, and Mary Eastwood of the Justice Department—displayed strong commitments to advancing women's rights. Along with ICSW Executive Secretary Catherine East of the Woman's Bureau, these women formed the basis of a small coterie of in-government feminists.

The 20 CAC members were Presidential appointees.[12] Many had served on the PCSW. Some represented a constituency: Marguerite Rawalt was a former national president of the Business and Professional Women; Viola Hymes had served in the same capacity for the National Council of Jewish Women; Dorothy Height was president of the National Council of Negro Women. Their appointments were personal and their representation unofficial, but their connections with these respectable organizations no doubt served as a restraint against any incipient radicalism. Other CAC members were chosen because friendship or reputation had proved them competent and trustworthy. One longtime friend of Johnson's believed she was appointed to the CAC because the President "wanted somebody that he trusted not to be too far out."[13]

As the eminently responsible women who composed the Status of Women groups came to see a need for changing women's status, they recognized a profound psychological difficulty: promoting their own interests seemed unfeminine. Women and women's organizations had a long and proud tradition of altruistic service, related to woman's role as caretaker and nurturer. Aggressive advocacy of their own interests would challenge the principles by which women defined themselves. President Johnson's interest in broadening women's role eased this problem for the federal Status of Women groups; they could advocate change for women simply by following the President's lead. He had publicly expressed his commitment to broadening and upgrading women's participation in American life, and he had demanded the appointment of more women to top-level government jobs. In personal appearances at several CAC meetings and national Status of Women conferences, he expressed a support that was reiterated in private communications. Esther Peterson felt confident of Johnson's backing.[14] In a January, 1965 memo to Wirtz, she noted her understanding that Johnson wished the work of the groups to "proceed full steam ahead."[15] Because advocating changes in women's status presented no conflicts with the loyalty expected of political appointees, the federal Status of Women groups were able to begin their work with confidence and to transmit some of their assurance to the state commissions.[16]

But the Status of Women groups had to convince other women, particularly those in the large, prestigious women's organizations, to join their efforts. At its October, 1964 meeting, the CAC discussed the need to motivate women to become more concerned with their status. The official summary of the meeting noted:

> Women's organizations hesitate to take the lead in correcting injustice because they may appear to be self-serving. It was suggested that women's organizations might be persuaded to take more leadership if it were taken in the context of our total concern for the rights of minorities. Mrs. [Viola] Hymes suggested that if women felt they were working to develop opportunities for others who were disadvantaged as well as [for] women, the role of advocate would be more acceptable.[17]

The CAC was moving away from the notion that sex and race were distinct forms of discrimination needing separate remedies. It was also developing a strategy to make women's advocacy of women's interests more acceptable, a strategy perfectly suited to the administration's War on Poverty.

The War on Poverty provided a logical vehicle for what would later be called "consciousness raising." As an altruistic undertaking, it attracted women's "natural" interests, carrying on the long-accepted tradition of women's involvement in social reform. More importantly, the problem of poverty had a special meaning for women; more women (14 million) lived in poverty than did men (10.5 million) or children under age 16 (also 10.5 million).[18]

In February, 1964, as the administration was formulating legislation for the poverty program, the CAC discussed the need for "creative planning" to deal with specifically female poverty.[19] The Council seems to have understood that lack of knowledge about women in poverty might skew the direction of the developing program; it noted the need for studies of young women similar to the one on draft rejectees undertaken by the President's Task Force on Manpower Conservation. That study, published as *One-Third of a Nation*, occasioned much consternation and discussion by revealing that a third of the young males registering for the draft were rejected on grounds of mental and physical deficiencies, and that most of these rejectees came from impoverished families.[20] Assuming that a demonstration of need would result in demands for remedial programs for young women as well as for young men, the CAC expressed what later appeared to be a naive faith in the War on Poverty rhetoric. The CAC's enthusiasm for participating in the War on Poverty reflected both its sense of identification with the Johnson administration and its desire to improve women's lot. At the time, these two aims did not appear to be in conflict.

Experiences with the poverty program raised women's consciousness in ways not foreseen by the CAC. The program's planners had not absorbed the new thinking about women's special needs developing within the Status of Women groups. Discovering the philosophy of the poverty program regarding women, and recognizing it as a threat was an early and important step in the development of a feminist consciousness.

That the War on Poverty *had* a philosophy on women was not immediately apparent, even to those who planned the legislation. In some ways it is inaccurate to ascribe any particular philosophy to the planners of the poverty program, for they represented varied, and often conflicting, points of view. Yet their ideas of women's role in American economic life as reflected in confidential policy papers and legislative proposals are, in hindsight, remarkably consistent: men should earn money; women should care for men and children.

The importance of the program planners' thinking was enhanced by the peculiar circumstances of the War on Poverty's creation. Undertaken on behalf of a group that had no lobby, and developed by experts working behind closed doors in the executive branch, the War on Poverty was not subject to the usual political pressures. At the time of Kennedy's death, the Council of Economic Advisors (CEA) and the Bureau of the Budget (BOB) had been working on antipoverty measures to present as part of Kennedy's 1964 legislative package. Told about these plans shortly after assuming office, Johnson responded, "That's my kind of program. . . .Move full speed ahead."[21]

In the early months of his tenure, Johnson desperately needed a campaign issue, a program to distinguish himself from Kennedy; the women-in-government campaign was a response to that need, but an attack on poverty was an infinitely more promising and politically appealing approach. Since poverty was a white as well as a black problem, an antipoverty program had great potential for defusing Southern rancor over the civil rights legislation Johnson intended to pass. A prosperous economy and a lack of distracting foreign problems made the time right for a major domestic undertaking. A crusade against mankind's ancient enemy, moreover, might capture the still unfocused idealism awakened by Kennedy. And what political opponent would dare speak in favor of poverty? The only problem was to get the program operating by the time of the election, so that the impact of Johnson's compassion would clearly be matched by the realization that he was a "can do" leader. Johnson embraced the idea so enthusiastically that he declared "unconditional war on poverty" in his first State of the Union address.[22]

In February he named Sargeant Shriver to direct the war. Shriver had won acclaim for his able management of another visionary, idealistic program, the Peace Corps; his ties to the Kennedy family (as the former President's brother-in-law) were a further asset. Given a billion dollar budget and very little time for program development, Shriver gathered a task force and drew up details for the antipoverty legislation, using the CEA and BOB's preliminary work as a basis, but making substantive changes.[23] The Economic Opportunity bill went to Congress in March, 1964, just six weeks after Shriver's appointment.

The bill's provisions constituted not so much a war on poverty in general as a war against specific types of poverty selected by the CEA-BOB group and Shriver's task force. Political concerns and the state of socio-logical knowledge served as the major influences in the task force's selections; neither factor suggested the need for specific remedies for female poverty. Throughout the planning process, for example, the poverty of female-headed families was viewed as a phenomenon related and secondary to the problem of male unemployment.

A CEA report prepared in December, 1963, describing the general outlines of an attack on poverty illustrates this point.[24] The report noted that of poor families:

—31% were headed by a person over 65 years old
—23% were headed by a female
—21% were nonwhite
—20% had three or more children.[25]

A chief problem of the first two groups was their "limited earning potential," related, in the case of female-headed families, to the lack of a "male breadwinner."[26] The report recognized discrimination as a factor in limiting employment opportunities and earnings for nonwhites, but women were not mentioned in this connection.[27] Rather than classifying female family heads with nonwhites, the report likened them to the aged, as persons for whom paid employment was, in most cases, not a socially desirable alternative. For these groups, the CEA recommended income supplements as the solution to poverty.[28]

The idea that mothers should be paid to stay home with their children began with the "mothers' pension" movement of the Progressive era, and lived on in the federal program for Aid to Families of Dependent Children which, despite its nomenclature, made payments chiefly to mothers. In practice, the payments had seldom been generous enough to relieve poverty, but the theory had an inescapable validity in the early twentieth century when most men were breadwinners and most women homemakers. By the 1960s, the patterns of men's and women's work had changed, but public perceptions had not. In accepting, uncritically, the traditional division of labor between the sexes, the CEA's thinking was in line with standard concepts of social desirability.

Shriver's task force, operating on a strict timetable and embroiled in inner-circle political and philosophical conflicts, had no reason to challenge the male-breadwinner/female-homemaker concept. It chose, almost automatically, to focus its efforts on males, believing that the problem of male unemployment was the most important component of the larger problem of poverty, and the one most susceptible to solution. Searching for a program which would show quick results, the task force developed the Job Corps as a star attraction of the War on Poverty.

Designed to recruit unemployable young men away from debilitating environments, teach them job skills and good work habits, and help them find jobs, the Job Corps was a modification of the Youth Employment-Youth Conservation Corps bill which passed the Senate in 1963 but stalled in the House Committee on Rules. Support for this bill came from a shaky coalition of conservationists who wanted to put unemployed youths to work on public projects similar to those undertaken by the New Deal's Civilian Conservation Corps, and welfare oriented groups hoping to ease the problems of youth unemployment and juvenile delinquency by providing job training and public works projects within urban communities. Urged on by Willard Wirtz, who foresaw Department of Labor control of the anticipated job training projects, Shriver's task force agreed with the welfare groups that rural conservation camps had little relevance to the unemployment problems of the 1960s, and designed the Job Corps to emphasize urban job training rather than rural public works. To keep enrollees in an urban setting and at the same time remove them from the environmental forces which seemed to discourage incentive, the planners developed the idea of urban residential training centers. Temporarily removed from their own communities, the Job Corpsmen would be placed in an environment designed to encourage and reward their efforts to extricate themselves from the cycle of poverty.

More than any of the other components of the poverty program, the Job Corps would be quick to show results. If it succeeded, it would justify the concept of the War on Poverty, build public support for greater efforts and larger appropriations, and greatly augment Lyndon Johnson's chances for election in his own right. The Job Corps' planners had an enormously complex system to put together, little time to do it, and immense pressure to make it a quick success. The first hurdle was winning Congressional approval of the poverty package.

The Economic Opportunity bill, as the package was called (to give it a more positive name), had its first hearings before the House Committee on Education and Labor, starting in March, 1964. Republican opponents on the committee were in a minority, and kept sharply in check by Chairman Adam Clayton Powell's maneuvering. But the support of key Democrats was crucial to the bill's later success on the House floor.

Edith Green was one of those key Democrats. Green had close ties to the Status of Women groups, having served on the PCSW. Barely a month before the poverty hearings began, she had been the only female Representative to side with the Women's Bureau in voting against the sex amendment to Title VII. At that time, Green had worried that she might be called an "Uncle Tom" or an "Aunt Jane" because of her position. Perhaps spurred on by a desire to clarify her support for women's rights, and certainly aided by her long-developed clout on the Committee, Green objected to the all-male nature of the Job Corps. She broached the subject on the first day of Committee hearings, when questioning Shriver and Secretary of Defense Robert McNamara. Their exchanges illustrate the dawning recognition of a conflict between the emerging feminist view and the establishment liberalism of the 1960s. Green began by repudiating the one remnant of American feminist tradition:

. . . I do not consider myself a suffragette, but I notice that the Jobs Corps part of the bill is limited to young men. Will you explain why this limitation is made?

. . . . .

Mr. Shriver. The principal purpose of these centers was to give young men, who we hope will be heads of families and wage earners, an opportunity. . .to learn the necessary skills. . .for employment during the rest of their lives. Now, this is not to say that women obviously don't need similar skills for employment, but it is thought at the beginning, there being so many young men in this age group 16 to 21, that we should start with them.

Mrs. Green. Are there not as many young women in that age group, or probably more because military service absorbs a large number of young men?

Mr. Shriver. There probably are. But the thought was to start with those who would have as their principle necessity in life. . .the earning of a living and supporting of a family. . . .[W]e started with the men because we felt that. . .the need was greatest there.

Mrs. Green. It seems to me that is in conflict with the recent emphasis that the President has placed on a more active role for women in our society. . . .

Mr. Shriver. . .[W]e would be very much interested if you felt that this legislation should be modified to establish some of these training. . .centers for women.

Mrs. Green. Let me repeat for the record that I certainly do feel that way.[29]

Secretary McNamara agreed that training for young girls was a "good idea" but asserted that the need for training "primary breadwinners" was "much greater." Green argued that his thinking was discriminatory:

. . .I will point out that one out of every three persons who today hold jobs in the United States is a woman. Furthermore, there are millions of women who are heads of families, yet they are paid less and they are given fewer opportunities. . . .
. . .We dare not suggest that the Job Corps be designed for individuals of a particular race or a particular creed. But this being a man's world, we unthinkingly design the Job Corps for men only. . . . It strikes in me an odd chord that, when we have a long-term basic remedial program, women are excluded from a vital section.[30]

The bill's sponsors were less than enthusiastic about Green's proposal. Realizing that they would have to make concessions to the advocates of rural conservation camps, the planners hoped to conserve as much of the Job Corps budget as possible for use on the urban centers, the ones most likely to show results.[31] Women's Centers would drain funds from the Job Corps' primary purpose, and add still further complications to a program already overburdened with political expectations. But Green's support was deemed necessary, and her logic was hard to fault. None of the administration witnesses at the hearings was so ungentlemanly as to argue that women should not have a share of the Job Corps funds, but Willard Wirtz, the chairman of the ICSW, offered the only outright espousal of Green's view.

Testifying in his capacity as Secretary of Labor, Wirtz diverged from his prepared statement to stress his Department's support:

> I should like to make clear, in view of the discussions which I know have taken place...before this committee, the significance which we attach to making it definitely certain that this attack on poverty will benefit the women of this country as well as the men. I think the country still realizes much too little of the growing importance of women as members of the work force and as heads of families.
>
> I think the country does not realize that in the manpower developments of the past twelve months, women played statistically a much larger part than the men. The country does not realize the extent to which women are today the heads of families, a high percentage of the families who are in a poverty status.[32]

Wirtz's support was no doubt helpful to Green, but it was her key position on the committee that led the bill's planners to accede to her demands. By the time the bill left the committee in May, Green had an "understanding" that women would constitute at least one third of the total enrollment.[33]

Wirtz and the ICSW were delighted with Green's success, but feared the informal one third quota would unfairly restrict young women's participation in the Job Corps.[34] Green, however, saw the quota as a guarantee that women would be included. Believing that the planners lacked concern for the plight of impoverished young women, she lamented that a specific quota had not been included in the legislation.[35]

Preparations for the men's Job Corps Centers were already underway when Green's amendment was accepted; if the Women's Centers were to begin operations simultaneously with the men's, planning had to begin before the bill's final passage. To direct the planning, Green recommended Dr. Jeanne Noble, a black associate professor of Human Relations at New York University. Since appropriations were not yet available, Noble became Interim Director of the Job Corps Task Force for Women's Training Centers without compensation. She gathered a staff of experts from universities, voluntary organizations such as the Girl Scouts, women in the armed services, and from the Office of Education and the Women's Bureau. Except for the few women on loan from executive departments, all task force members served without pay; many took leaves of absence from their regular jobs. Noble later complained that "for many of the staff, poverty became a personal phenomenon."[36] Since Shriver's task force was almost entirely composed of persons on loan from government agencies or well-financed private foundations, its members did not have to deal with this problem.[37]

Statistical information on the young women who might be helped by the Women's Job Corps was practically nonexistent; Noble's task force asked for help from the Women's Bureau, which supplied compendia of what information could be found or estimated, "Who Are the Young Girls

16-19 Years of Age?" and "Women in Poverty."[38] There was ample evidence of the existence of poverty and lack of employment skills among young women; an estimated half-million girls formed the target population. But because female drop outs had received neither the popular nor scholarly attention devoted to male juvenile delinquents, no conception had developed as to what sort of help these women wanted or what kinds of training would be most helpful to them. With the role of women in the larger society in a state of flux, setting desirable goals for young women in poverty was a challenging process.

One special concern of Noble's task force was the growing number of poor families headed by women. Between 1948 and 1960, the number of poor, female-headed families rose by 19 percent, while the total number of poor families actually decreased by 22 percent.[39] This trend was ominous, for the incidence of poverty in female-headed families was nearly 50 percent. The situation was particularly severe for black female family heads: 75 percent were poor. A task force working paper enumerated some of the problems faced by daughters in these poor and fatherless families:

> [Especially for illegitimate children,] the impact on the mother's feelings often blights the necessary process of sexual identification and distorts the child's image of the husband-wife relationship into the patterns that so often prompt promiscuity, delinquency and anti-social behavior...In many of these mother-only families (23% of white, and 61% of non-white) mothers work full time and because of their meagre incomes cannot provide satisfactory supervision and day care of children. Caring for the younger children frequently falls to the older daughters and further restricts their chances for educational advancement.[40]

To help the daughters avoid a repetition of this cycle, the Women's Job Corps Program would focus on personal enrichment and "education for home and family life," as well as on the development of vocational skills.

To get broader input and public attention for the Women's Job Corps, the task force sponsored a conference in July attended by nearly 100 persons. Community organizers, leaders of women's organizations, and experts in health and education travelled to Washington at their own expense to offer advice and cooperation. As an outgrowth of the conference, preparations were begun for a special network of volunteers to screen recruits for the centers. With encouragement from Mrs. Johnson and assistance from the Women's Bureau, four national organizations—the National Councils of Catholic, Jewish, and Negro Women, and the United Church Women—formed Women in Community Service (WICS). By 1967, WICS had 114 recruiting centers located throughout the country.[41] Ultimately, the WICS volunteers were unable to supply all the female recruits, and by 1968 the U.S. Employment Service, which had been screening all the male recruits, agreed to supply half of the female enrollees. But WICS played an important role in developing and broadening support for the Women's Job Corps program.[42] The YWCA, too, expressed its support by agreeing to operate a Women's Center in Los Angeles, and by offering special assistance to Job Corps graduates living in YWCA residence halls.[43] This sort of involvement by women's organizations was exactly what the CAC had hoped to encourage.

As plans were being formulated, the number of females to be enrolled the first year continued to be a matter of concern and controversy. At the July conference, Noble announced that enrollment in the Women's Centers would be no more than one-third of the total. According to Women's Bureau Director Mary Dublin Keyserling, Noble felt she had to accept that quota "without question."[44] Edith Green understood that Shriver's aides favored an enrollment of only 2,000 women, one-twentieth of the proposed total.[45] At Keyserling's request, Wirtz wrote to Shriver, expressing the ICSW's view that restrictive quotas should not be imposed on female enrollment in the Jobs Corps.[46] Shriver's response pointed out that estimates of the number of female enrollees were necessary for budgetary planning, but were not intended to restrict enrollment. The number of qualified volunteers would determine future plans, and might result in a division of "50/50 or any other combination." Shriver contended that Noble had supplied the figure used for developing the first year's budget: 6600 girls, or about one-sixth of the proposed total.[47]

On August 20, Johnson signed the Economic Opportunity Act at a ceremony in his office. There, Green learned that Shriver's task force, now being reorganized as the Office of Economic Opportunity (OEO), had made a "firm decision" on the one-sixth ratio. Reporting this news to Wirtz, Keyserling said, "Edith Green feels she has been sold down the river." Nor was that the end of the bad news; women were being ignored in the OEO's organization. "I am told," Keyserling continued,

> Jeanne Noble is being pushed far down the line in the administrative structure. There are no women, as far as we can find out, being appointed at the top decision making level.
> My own feeling is that there ought to be strong representation, not only from the ICSW, but also from national [women's] organizations. This is the President's program. Perhaps he should be informed. . . .[48]

India Edwards did write the President, protesting the one-sixth quota and the "down-grading" of the Women's Job Corps, but to no avail.[49] When appropriations for the OEO became available in October, the women who had volunteered their services to Noble's task force for over four months were designated mere "temporary consultants." Before offering her own resignation, Noble recommended that they be given permanent staff positions to relieve unnecessary anxiety and improve morale.[50]

Women who worked to develop the Women's Job Corps program were deeply frustrated by the subtle opposition they encountered. The OEO was obviously not taking their concerns seriously, but since the reasons for this attitude were unclear, and the attitude itself not publicly acknowledged, it was difficult to attack. That difficulty was removed the following summer (1965) with publication of the Moynihan Report, which, quite unintentionally, revealed a male bias that seemed to explain the OEO's lack of enthusiasm for the Women's Job Corps. The report was an important catalyst in crystallizing the definition of women's interests developing within the Status of Women organizations, for it advocated a policy which these women perceived as threatening.

The report's author, Daniel Patrick Moynihan, had been a key planner on Shriver's Task Force, having special responsibility for the Job Corps and other training programs.[51] After returning to his duties as Assistant Secretary of Labor for Policy Planning and Research, Moynihan began a search for new ways to attack "the Negro problem." Studying census data, he was struck by the fact that most black children did not live continuously with both parents. Further investigation convinced him that among lower-class blacks, family structure was in a state of acute crisis.

Moynihan outlined his thesis in a January, 1965 memo to presidential aide Bill Moyers. Explaining that, for historical reasons, black family structure had never been strong, Moynihan argued that it was now seriously deteriorating because of high rates of unemployment among black males and governmental policies such as AFDC regulations which encouraged female-headed households. The weakened stature and authority of the black male, he warned, had created a "pathological matriarchal situation which is beginning to feed on itself." He urged that the federal government turn its attention to strengthening the black family as a way of handling the problems of unemployment and poverty at their source. By strengthening the black family, Moynihan meant boosting the status of the black male as provider and breadwinner. "Negro males," he wrote, "is where the problem is."

Moynihan offered no specific details for a solution to the crisis he perceived, but relayed the comment of a "distinguished Negro sociologist" with whom he had discussed what might be done to help black males. The sociologist

> did not know what if anything could be done, but he was sure of one thing. Anything that could be done to hurt the Negro woman would help. He was not smiling.[52]

In May, Wirtz forwarded Moynihan's completed position paper to the President, calling it "nine pages of dynamite about the Negro situation."[53] Moynihan warned Johnson that the civil rights movement, having achieved legislative guarantees of equal opportunity, was moving into a new phase. Soon its leaders would be expecting equality of *results*, and these were not likely to be forthcoming. Despite the growth of a black middle class, the situation of lower-class blacks was deteriorating so seriously that equal opportunity would not bring about equal rights. The principal reason for the deterioration, Moynihan asserted, was the disorganization of the Negro family structure caused by the "systematic weakening of the position of the Negro male."[54] He urged adoption of a governmental policy to "bring the structure of the Negro family into line with that of the rest of our society." Among his specific suggestions were reform of the welfare system and the creation of more jobs for men, "even if we have to displace some females."[55]

Moynihan advised Johnson, then riding the crest of his popularity and power, to "leapfrog" the civil rights movement; instead of waiting for the customary buildup of demands, with eventual government response, Johnson could assume leadership of the new phase of the quest for equality. This is what Johnson attempted to do in a major policy speech delivered at Howard University in June, 1965. The Howard speech was a broad assessment of the state of equality, relating what had been accomplished and suggesting what still remained to be done. Johnson mentioned the problems of the black family only in general terms, relating them to "the devastating heritage of long years of slavery, and a century of oppression, hatred, and injustice."[56] He did not mention matriarchy as a problem, nor did he advocate displacing women from their jobs. He did, however, forward the idea that equal results were a legitimate aim of public policy.

Initial reaction to the Howard speech was favorable, and in July, the Department of Labor released Moynihan's report to the public as one of its official publications, under the title *The Negro Family: the Case for National Action*.[57] Moynihan's earlier statements were considerably softened and qualified. The report argued that there was nothing intrinsically wrong with a "matriarchal" society, but that such a setup was dysfunctional for American blacks.

[I]t is clearly a disadvantage for a minority group to be operating on one principle, while the majority of the population, and the one with the most advantages to begin with, is operating on another.... Ours is a society which presumes male leadership in private and public affairs. The arrangements of society facilitate such leadership and reward it.[58]

From a feminist viewpoint, such as was beginning to develop within the Status of Women groups, there was much to argue with in the report. The conclusions which Moynihan drew from statistics about fatherless families, for example, were in marked contrast to those reached by Noble's task force. The choice of the term "matriarchy," connoting emasculating control and power, was particularly inept and unfortunate. The idea that families could be strengthened by putting the woman "in her place" to boost the man's status was certainly open to question. Moreover, Moynihan's view of white middle-class family structure as a static system in which men were bread-winners and women homemakers was out of date.

The report aroused a great controversy, but not for any of the above reasons. A few lonely voices spoke out in defense of the black woman,[59] but the protest came chiefly from civil rights leaders who resented the statement that black males and black families were weak. The report attributed that weakness to past circumstances and present policies, but movement leaders charged that the argument was merely a more sophisticated form of the old idea that blacks were inferior. Viewing black family structure as the problem, they argued, implied that black people themselves, rather than the social and economic setup, were responsible for their situation. Such conclusions were far from Moynihan's intention, but the outcry continued. Bureaucratic opposition to changes in the welfare structure suggested by the report added to the political furor, as did five days of severe rioting in the black Watts community of Los Angeles in August. Moynihan contended that the riots proved his point that "things were going to hell at the bottom,"[60] but political fallout from the riot placed the administration in a delicate situation *vis à vis* civil rights leaders, and Moynihan dutifully resigned.[61]

As the basis for any immediate policy initiatives, the Moynihan report was dead, but its thesis concerning the desirable role of black women had not been repudiated. The Women's Bureau moved to refute some of Moynihan's points when it sponsored, in conjunction with the National Council of Negro Women, a November conference on "The Negro Woman in the USA; New Roles in Family and Community Life."[62] Keyserling's keynote speech stressed that employment problems would not be solved by taking much-needed jobs away from women and giving them to men. "There must," she said, "be jobs for all who need and want to work."[63] WB publications continued to point out that black women had lower average earnings and higher general unemployment rates than black males, yet the idea persisted that black women were somehow a hindrance to their race's quest for economic equality. Two years after Moynihan resigned, Martha Griffiths complained to Wirtz that the report had convinced "intelligent and usually well-informed people" that "Negro women have it good." Griffiths was particularly distressed by a "scurrilous article" in *Parade Magazine* (an insert carried in many Sunday newspapers) titled "Negro Problem: Women Rule the Roost."[64]

Because it was a widely known public document that articulated the generally unspoken assumption of the civil rights movement that black women should "stand behind" their men, i.e., know their place, the Moynihan report eventually became a favorite target of feminist attack.[65] But in the summer of 1965, feminism was not yet an acceptable point of view. There were, however, indications that an increasing number and variety of women were beginning to look seriously and critically at their condition as women. Betty Friedan's *The Feminine Mystique*, a lament to the wasted talents and frustrated lives of middle-class housewives, published in 1963 to a lukewarm response, was released in paperback in 1964 and was on its way to becoming a best seller. To whatever insights may have been achieved through Friedan's book, and the less widely dispersed but politically important educational efforts of the various Status of Women groups, was now added the impact of Moynihan's bald statement that power in American society was a male prerogative.

The short shrift given to the Women's Job Corps began to make sense in light of the Moynihan report. To women sensitized by their work on the Status of Women groups, it appeared that the OEO had already decided to "reestablish the male as head of the house" by keeping women's participation in the War on Poverty at a minimum.[66]

Moynihan's report, by clearly spelling out existing biases and suggesting policies that would deprive the poorest of women of opportunities for self-support (albeit with the hope that men would then support them), forced a greater awareness of the pervasive effect of sex discrimination on women of every race and economic class. To be sure, the effects of sex discrimination differed greatly according to class and race, and continued attention to these factors would be necessary, but the idea was gaining credence that women shared a common plight and a common interest that cut across traditional forms of classification. Advocacy of women's equality thus appeared less selfish, and the role of advocate more "appropriate" for women. The nature of the public response to the Moynihan report clearly indicated that women would not be able to rely on anyone but themselves to fill that role.

This recognition developed as the administration's support for improving women's opportunities seemed to be waning. Johnson had made no announced change in his opinions, but had greatly de-emphasized his efforts on women's behalf. He had, moreover, apparently been willing to sanction Moynihan's policy suggestions until they became too sensitive politically. The OEO, too, appeared to subscribe to the viewpoint that males should be helped at the expense of females. And as the Moynihan controversy was still brewing, an even more ominous threat appeared as the Equal Employment Opportunity Commission (EEOC), the agency created to enforce Title VII of the Civil Rights Act, began to formulate policy for dealing with sex discrimination.

Response to the EEOC's early policy formulations, which will be discussed in the next chapter, shows that the experience with the Women's Job Corps and the lessons of the Moynihan report had influenced attitudes at least among the leaders of the Status of Women organizations. A small but influential group of women was beginning to understand what was at stake if women were not specifically included in governmental programs to promote equal opportunity.

6

Equality vs. Protection Revisited, 1964–1966

Difficulties in establishing a Women's Job Corps and discovery of an antifemale bias in the Moynihan Report sparked a new feminist consciousness among members of Status of Women organizations and others interested in expanding women's opportunities. The feminist outlook became even more clearly defined as women attempted to influence policies for implementing the sex provision in Title VII of the Civil Rights Act of 1964. United in a desire to improve women's employment opportunities, defenders of women's interests were still plagued by the old division of opinion over the desirability of women's protective laws. As the fight over the Equal Rights Amendment entered its fifth decade, the conflict between protection and equality had been neither resolved nor suppressed, nor had it succeeded in exciting wide political interest. Protectionists, led by Esther Peterson, appeared to be gaining some ground in 1964, when the terms of the debate suddenly shifted. The sex amendment to Title VII gave a new and more vital form to the debate.

This chapter, after looking at the status of the ERA at the time of Title VII's passage, will explore the ways in which Title VII revised the terms of the debate between equality and protection, and examine the circumstances which led to the first major political battle for the new feminists, their fight with the Equal Employment Opportunity Commission.

In 1964, for the first time in two decades, the Democratic platform did not include an equal rights plank. It was a victory for Esther Peterson who failed to keep the equal rights issue out of Kennedy's platform four years earlier.[1] The 1963 report of the President's Commission on the Status of Women, which concluded that a constitutional amendment "need not now be sought," provided a justification for omitting the ERA from the 1964 platform.[2] In the summer of 1964, as additional protection, the Women's Bureau quietly "gave assistance to representatives of a large number of national organizations" who planned to testify before platform committees of both parties in support of the Bureau's traditional anti-ERA position.[3]

Peterson's cause received a further boost from President Johnson's desire to control the contents of "his" platform. Attempting to reconcile his conflicting needs for a united convention and a strong civil rights platform, Johnson decided to draw up the platform he wanted and then persuade delegates to accept it without major revisions. Administration officials compiled the platform in Washington well in advance of the August convention in Atlantic City. Secretary of Labor Willard Wirtz, who shared Peterson's antipathy toward the ERA, wrote the sections relevant to women's rights; his draft made no mention of equal legal rights for women either by constitutional amendment or legislation, but focused instead on the Kennedy-Johnson achievement in expanding employment opportunities for women.[4]

Convention leaders at Atlantic City allowed few changes in Johnson's prepackaged platform. An ERA plank, introduced by National Women's Party leader Emma Guffey Miller, was defeated, causing ERA proponents to complain that the Platform Committee was stacked against them. The only apparent repercussions from this episode were a few letters of complaint sent to the President by the small band of ERA supporters. One letter stated that some convention delegates attributed the ERA's exclusion to "*the White House, itself*," but Esther Peterson received most of the blame. An ERA "veteran" charged that Peterson had been "sent. . .by Walter Reuther [leader of the United Auto Workers] to get the Equal Rights Amendment planks out of both [party] platforms." Emma Guffey Miller complained to Johnson that "many thousands of Democratic women" questioned Peterson's right to "dictate the woman's plank."[5]

Yet to Peterson, the 1964 platform was more a relief than a cause for celebration. She opposed the ERA primarily on the assumption that it would invalidate a series of state laws designed to protect women by regulating the wages, hours, and conditions under which they could work. But the Civil Rights Act of 1964, signed by President Johnson in July (just a month before the convention) presented a new and more serious threat to women's protective legislation. Intending to nullify state laws permitting racial employment discrimination, authors of the Civil Rights Act included a section (708) specifically stating that compliance with state laws was not an admissible excuse for violating Title VII's antidiscrimination provision. Once sex was added to the bases upon which employment discrimination was prohibited, any state employment laws discriminating on the basis of sex were likewise nullified. Although the legislative history gave no concise indication of Congressional intent regarding protective laws, the testimony from both opponents of "restrictions" and supporters of "protections" suggested that they would be invalidated. More to the point, a literal reading of Title VII clearly threatened their legality.

The matter hinged on a legal question: were protective laws discriminatory? They fit the standard definition of discrimination by singling out women as a class for special treatment, but unlike laws permitting racial segregation, women's protective laws were widely viewed as having a favorable effect on the group they regulated. A series of Supreme Court decisions, beginning with *Muller* v. *Oregon* in 1908, upheld the view that protections for working women promoted the public interest and established sex as a valid basis for legal classifications. These rulings suggested that protective laws might not be discriminatory according to the language and intent of the new law. The question would have to be resolved by the agency created to enforce Title VII, the Equal Employment Opportunity Commission (EEOC).

The legal problem was complicated by political considerations. An interpretation of women's protective laws as discriminatory would repudiate a long-standing Women's Bureau policy of encouraging such laws. While recommending their ultimate extension to workers of both sexes, the PCSW, too, affirmed its support for strengthening existing protections to working women. Lack of Congressional committee hearings on the sex provision, moreover, had denied supporters of protectionism, such as the AFL-CIO, an opportunity to express their views. A major change in federal policy toward these state laws was unthinkable without further political discussion.

Broader questions of social policy were also involved, for legal restrictions on women's participation in the workforce reflected society's attitudes toward women's other roles. Protective laws were an attempt to reconcile the fact of women's labor force participation with the idea that women's primary responsibilities were to home and family. Supporters of equal rights for women, such as the National Women's Party, contended that the philosophy of protectionism perpetuated women's status as second-class citizens, and argued that only by receiving identical treatment in the workplace could women begin to move toward equality with men.

Despite dramatic changes in women's labor force participation neither side of the argument had changed significantly since the debate began in the 1920s. But Title VII's linkage of sex and race discrimination cast the issue in a new light by placing the issue of women's employment opportunities in the context of a debate whose terms were well understood. Race discrimination was the chief political issue of the mid-1960s; widespread and heated public debate had made most Americans conscious of the basic issues involved in the struggle for black equality. Arguments advanced to upgrade the status of blacks could also apply to women: both groups were subject to prejudicial, stereotyped assumptions that relegated their members to low paying, low status jobs. Viewed in this context, any legal constraints on women's economic advancement appeared unfair to individual women and detrimental to the national interest.

Comparison of sex and race as factors influencing employment status downplayed the significance of women's roles outside the workplace, a major concern of both the Women's Bureau and the PCSW. This linkage further obscured the fact that all the rules by which the workplace operated—from hours of work to patterns of advancement—were designed for workers with *wives* to provide supportive services and take care of family needs. Even the cautious Women's Bureau did not appear to recognize the revolutionary implications of linking race and sex discrimination; its earlier opposition to the connection stemmed from the view that racial discrimination was the more serious problem. In defending protective laws, the Bureau stressed that women workers were a special case by virtue of their family and household responsibilities, but its primary emphasis was on alleviating exploitation of lower-class working women who lacked the protection of unions, and were typically not employed in jobs covered by federal Fair Labor Standards laws. The implication that more comprehensive legislation and higher incomes would solve any problems peculiar to women workers was strengthened by WB recommendations that executive, administrative, and professional positions be exempted from state protective laws. But the conflict between discrimination and protection, as Americans would discover over the following decades, went far beyond the concerns of laundry workers and domestics, reaching into the structure of the most basic economic and social institutions: workplace and family.

Well in advance of Title VII's July 1965 effective date, the Women's Bureau began to seek ways to influence Equal Employment Opportunity Commission policies. A series of recommendations from federal Status of Women groups was the most obvious way to influence the new agency, but disagreement over the proper policies to recommend quickly became apparent. In January, 1965, Bureau officials discussed plans for the Interdepartmental Committee on the Status of Women (ICSW) to submit a policy paper to the EEOC, outlining "implications of various interpretive issues" involved in enforcing the sex clause.[6] In February ICSW Chairman Wirtz appointed a committee to draft such a paper for ICSW approval. The three committee members were in general agreement that Title VII's exempting clauses should be narrowly construed, giving the new law a broad application, but despite repeated attempts to reach agreement, they remained deadlocked on the issue of state protective laws.[7] Not until May, as the new EEOC was being appointed, did the committee make its final report, and it was inconclusive. WB Director Mary Dublin Keyserling, reflecting traditional Department of Labor support for protective laws, claimed that they presented no conflict with Title VII. The other two committee members, Mary Eastwood of the Justice Department, and Evelyn Harrison of the Civil Service Commission, argued that certain protective laws did discriminate against women and that employers covered by Title VII should be "relieved from compliance" with them.[8] Unable to secure an ICSW consensus, Wirtz sent a Department of Labor policy paper to the EEOC in August. Circumstances surrounding the sex amendment's passage, Wirtz argued, suggested no cause for a "general invalidation of these laws, many of which are useful and readily reconcilable with the purpose and objective of Title VII." He urged the EEOC to adopt a "policy of protecting and preserving these laws whenever possible and practicable."[9] The ICSW, for the time being, remained silent.

The newly appointed EEOC was in a delicate position. Lacking such conventional enforcement remedies as the power to issue cease and desist orders, it had to rely upon investigation and conciliation procedures to undo patterns of employment discrimination that had persisted for generations. To maximize its moral authority, the EEOC needed to win respect and voluntary cooperation from the business community while still maintaining support from the broad-based civil rights coalition that insured its continued existence. It needed also to convince Congress to appropriate funds sufficient for its operation, and to dispose legislators eventually to authorize extension of its powers. On top of all this, the EEOC had to interpret the unresolved problems of the sex provision, a part of the law passed in the distinct absence of public pressure.

A literal interpretation of the sex provision appeared so radical, so contrary to established social policy and business practice, that serious attempts to enforce it would surely harm the EEOC's precarious image. On its face, the law forbade employers, unions, and employment agencies from discriminating on the basis of sex in any action involving hiring, firing, training or promotion, unless a "bona fide occupational qualification" (*bfoq*) could be proved. If the *bfoq* exception were interpreted narrowly, indicating that sex was a legitimate qualification for relatively few jobs, the effect of the sex provision would indeed be radical. Ending job discrimination against blacks presented a formidable challenge, and blacks comprised only eleven percent of the 1964 labor force. Black and white women, on the other hand, constituted fully a third of the nation's workers.[10] And while the movement to end job discrimination against black males enjoyed a modicum of political support, sexual segregation of jobs was an unchallenged axiom of American business practice.

There were more immediate complications. Besides jeopardizing women's protective laws, a literal reading of Title VII would also necessitate a complete revamping of the way companies advertised for employees. Title VII required an end to classified job advertising in newspapers under columns headed "colored" and "white"; the sex amendment extended this prohibition to categorization of jobs under "male" and "female" headings as well. This consideration was particularly troublesome to the EEOC, for it aroused the ire of newspaper publishers, whose access to channels of public opinion gave them political clout. Literal enforcement of the sex provision was unthinkable under the circumstances, and since racial discrimination was clearly the target of its enabling legislation, the EEOC began by devoting its energies to that main assignment.

Initial reaction to the sex provision ranged from a sense of confusion within the EEOC to outright hostility among some affected groups. In July, 1965, the Illinois Chamber of Commerce asked for repeal of the sex provision; employers and unions, the Chamber said, were perplexed over its effects on Illinois laws regulating women's working hours and on differences in fringe benefits based on sex. EEOC Chairman Franklin D. Roosevelt, Jr., responded diplomatically that "the whole issue of sex discrimination is terribly complicated."[11] Some Commission employees resented having to deal with sex discrimination when more pressing matters needed their attention. Talk of repeal was soon joined by efforts to ridicule the sex provision. A derisive story that the law might require Playboy Clubs to hire male "bunnies" began to circulate through Washington offices and the sex provision became known as the "bunny law."[12] The bunny joke's appearance coincided closely with the release of Moynihan's report, increasing fears that administration support for women's advancement was on the wane.

Concern over the EEOC's attitude was evident at the second national conference of leaders of state Commissions on the Status of Women which met in Washington in July. EEOC Chairman Roosevelt and Aileen Hernandez, the only female among the five new Commissioners, addressed the conference; both sought to repudiate the notion that the EEOC would regard sex discrimination lightly. Said Roosevelt,

> If you have sensed a tendency on the part of some businessmen, government officials, and others to regard [the sex provisions of Title VII] as either frightening or humorous, let me assure you that I do not consider them in this light.[13]

Hernandez, a black, Republican, former official of the California Human Relations Commission, presented a more positive approach. Arguing that Title VII could become "an emancipation act for men," she wondered why men would not be offered the same protections as women.

> Why not a rest period for men? Don't they get tired too? Why not a weight restriction on the things they have to lift—have you looked at some of the figures on the incidence of hernia in men?
> ...Maybe there IS a "male bunny" who would like to be in a Playgirl Club. If we girls get to go to one of these clubs we might like to see a man.
> I know there has been a lot of levity...but it is not a funny subject. It has a very serious potential.[14]

Roosevelt further attempted to allay fears by announcing his agreement with the Labor Department's position on protective laws. Noting that the EEOC did "not see any clear Congressional intent to overturn all of these laws," he pledged it would "move with great care in taking any action which might affect their scope." He commended state Commissions' efforts to make protective laws "more up-to-date and more flexible;" this approach, he suggested, could "do much to clear up possible inconsistencies between outmoded laws and the purpose of Title VII."[15]

While alleviating some members' fears about the fate of protective laws, Roosevelt's speech raised yet another indication of trouble ahead by questioning whether sex-segregated classified job advertising was discriminatory.[16] Its status was similar to that of state protective laws in that neither topic had been considered in committee hearings; yet neither WB nor ICSW had considered sex-segregated advertising a matter for debate. Agreeing with a literal interpretation of the law on this point, Status of Women groups were apparently surprised to find sex-segregated advertising being discussed as one of the law's interpretive problems; they assumed it was patently forbidden by the language of Title VII.

Concerned about EEOC wavering on advertising policy, and fearful that frivolous references to "bunny" problems would undermine the law's enforcement, the Citizens Advisory Council appointed a committee to draft policy recommendations for the EEOC.[17] Both sides of the disagreement over protective labor laws were represented on this committee, but CAC Chairman Margaret Hickey "deliberately played down" that dispute to enable the Council to reach quick agreement on matters that appeared more pressing.[18] As finally drafted, the position paper disposed of the thorny problem of protective laws, which had kept the ICSW from developing any position paper at all, with a bland statement of support for the PCSW position taken in 1963 before the sex amendment had even been contemplated. The CAC was thus free to emphasize points on which all its members agreed: the sex provision should be treated seriously, and the ban on separate help-wanted advertising should be enforced.

In August, as CAC's draft policy paper was being prepared, new threats to serious enforcement of the sex provision arose from press coverage of the White House Conference on Equal Employment Opportunity. The Conference, required by Title VII, was designed to allow leaders of affected groups to become familiar with the law's provisions, and to enable these leaders to share their "practical comment and counsel" with the EEOC Commissioners and staff.[19] A panel discussion devoted to sex discrimination indicated that the EEOC was indeed anxious for such counsel, for it had not yet reached decisions on a number of major issues, including separate lines of seniority and differential provisions for men's and women's retirement and fringe benefits.[20]

Yet conference discussion did offer some positive guidance to firms covered by the law. It was unlawful, Commission representatives said, to limit executive training programs to males because of a supposition that women tended to leave employment more frequently than men. Employers were also warned that they bore responsibility for deciding whether to hire women for jobs traditionally held by men. Responding to a query from a railroad official who wondered if he would have to hire female locomotive engineers, Richard K. Berg, EEOC Deputy General Counsel, answered that if companies "can't think of any reason" not to hire women for such jobs, "then they better do it."[21]

Berg also confronted the reverse problem of a man applying for a job traditionally reserved for women by warning that the "bunny problem" was more than a joke. "The bunny question is interesting," Berg said, "because everybody [assuming the *bfoq* exemption would apply] considers the answer to be obvious. . . .But in terms of what bunnies do, it is something else—they serve drinks."[22]

The job description for bunnies actually included more than serving drinks; attractive women dressed in brief costumes featuring bunny tails and bunny ears were an integral part of the controlled yet sexually suggestive ambiance of Playboy Clubs which is best described as that of a brothel without a second floor. (In an actual brothel the applicability of the *bfoq* exemption would be beyond question.) Female gender, physical beauty, and sexual attractiveness, it could be argued, *were* reasonably necessary to the performance of the job of a bunny, but were the same characteristics necessary for airline stewardesses, waitresses, receptionists, and secretaries? The bunny problem was not as frivolous as the Status of Women groups imagined, for it highlighted a type of discrimination experienced commonly and almost exclusively by women. Although preferential hiring of young, sexually attractive women was widespread, neither the general public nor the Status of Women groups perceived this practice as a detriment to women's economic advancement.

The lack of an established feminist viewpoint helps explain the groups' failure to take the bunny problem seriously. Having just begun to recognize some of the political hurdles to be overcome for such a seemingly innocuous program as the Women's Job Corps, the Status of Women groups had not been forced to consider the relationship between society's attitudes toward female sexuality and women's economic opportunities. Another inhibiting factor may have been the impact of the racial parallel on thoughts about equal opportunity. The comparison between race discrimination and sex discrimination was obvious in the matter of segregated help-wanted ads (to Status of Women groups, if not necessarily to the EEOC), but similarities between a Playboy bunny and an "Uncle Tom" were not so easily discerned. The bunny problem, moreover, originated as a joke, and women's perception of it as an attempt to discredit the sex provision was probably accurate.

Deputy Counsel Berg's remarks at the White House Conference displayed sensitivity to the issue, but their publication on the front page of the *New York Times* created a sense of crisis among the defenders of women's interests. The *Times'* article marked the first important press attention given to the sex provision since the debate over its addition to the Civil Rights bill. Though the article itself was noninflammatory, its headline—"For Instance, Can She Pitch for the Mets?"—carried a derisive connotation that was more fully developed in a *Times* editorial the following day, August 21. Perhaps, the editors speculated, "it would have been better if Congress had just abolished sex itself," for now

> everything has to be neuterized. Housemaid becomes a dirty word; it is, of course, discriminatory. Handyman must disappear from the language; he was pretty much a goner anyways, if you ever started looking for one in desperation. . . .Girl Friday is an intolerable offense. . . .The Rockettes may be bi-sexual, and a pity, too. . . .Bunny problem, indeed! This is revolution, chaos. You can't even safely advertise for a wife anymore.[23]

One ICSW member later charged that the *Times* reported the White House Conference "as though it were the opening night of the latest Neil Simon comedy."[24] Esther Peterson, who argued against sex's inclusion in Title VII only eighteen months earlier, now took public action in its support. In a letter to the *Times'* editor, published September 3, she chided the paper for not treating the ban on sex discrimination in employment with "the seriousness it merits," and listed some of the pertinent questions the *Times* was avoiding.

> Why are women generally in the lowest paid jobs?. . . .How many jobs are "women's jobs" merely because they are menial, routine, monotonous and, of course, low-paying?

Peterson tried to defuse some of the *Times'* charges. She explained that because of the *bfoq* exemption, the bunny problem was "no problem at all." Further, she noted,

> the law does not even remotely suggest a "neuterization." Nor does it prohibit advertising for a wife—if that should be the way of romance.[25]

Intensified exposure of the bunny joke made the CAC's position paper more timely than its drafters had at first supposed; need for an official statement to counterbalance the unfavorable publicity seemed even more urgent after the White House Conference. By the end of September, CAC members had approved the draft and Chairman Hickey sent it to the ICSW. Overlooking its previous problems regarding protective laws, the ICSW endorsed the CAC's position paper and forwarded it to the EEOC in October.[26] The paper thus constituted an official policy statement approved by all the Presidentially appointed defenders of women's interests.

Recommendations to the EEOC developed in the paper placed primary emphasis on the "need for a positive approach" in enforcing the sex provision. "[C]oncentration on various odd and hypothetical cases," the paper complained, obscured the real and more common problems of sex discrimination, e.g., refusal to hire a woman based on assumptions about women's higher rates of absenteeism and turnover, or because of stereotyped characterizations about the differing physical capabilities of the sexes. Emphasis on the difficulties of interpretation, the paper continued, "gives the impression that enforcement may be delayed indefinitely and that compliance is not required." A positive approach was especially important to black women who, as victims of both race and sex discrimination, experienced a higher unemployment rate and lower average earnings than any other group. In a thinly veiled rebuttal of Moynihan's thesis, the CAC held that

> the anti-discrimination provisions of Title VII regarding sex can creatively reinforce those relating to race, color, religion and national origin. Our struggle against any one injustice need not dilute our efforts to eliminate the others. According broader employment opportunities to Negro men, for example, does not require the lessening of opportunities for women, including Negro women, but rather an expansion of opportunity for all.[27]

The paper also took a strong stand on the matter of sex-segregated help-wanted advertising in newspapers, expressing "alarm" at the "lack of compliance" with Title VII's provisions. Separate columns for men and women perpetuated discrimination by advising job applicants "not to apply where they are not wanted" and by encouraging "employers to place a sex label on jobs." Citing examples of newspapers that had combined their column headings to comply with antidiscrimination laws in Arizona and Hawaii, the CAC suggested that "adoption ... of a firm position on advertising would yield ready cooperation from the newspapers."[28]

By the time these recommendations reached the EEOC in October, it had already adopted a policy on sex-segregated job advertising. It would, "for the convenience of readers," allow employers to place ads in separate "male" and "female" columns as long as a notice in a prominent place on each page of such advertising stated that employers covered by Title VII could not discriminate on the basis of sex unless the *bfoq* applied to the particular job.[29] (See Appendix B for full policy statement.) The allowance of separate listings with a disclaimer was in marked contrast to the EEOC's flat prohibition of advertisements listed in racially separate columns. Both interpretations were based on the same statutory language, which provided no justification for differential policies.

As with the problem of protective laws, the EEOC's dilemma over advertising policy was political as well as legal. Title VII gave the EEOC no powers to regulate classified advertising; its authority extended only to businesses covered by Title VII which placed employment advertisements in newspapers. Publishers generally cooperated with the law by discontinuing help-wanted columns headed "white" or "colored" because the intensive campaign of civil rights advocates had educated the majority of them and their readers to the social benefits of doing so. But neither readers nor publishers had been forced to question the wisdom of separate "male" and "female" job advertisements. Some publishers claimed they lost revenue from employers who feared using racially neutral job advertisements; they anticipated an agonized outcry from their advertising clients if sex-segregated columns were discontinued. Through the American Newspaper Publishers Association they attempted to influence EEOC policy, hoping to save themselves from the trouble and expense of implementing a change for which they could see no rationale. In the face of this opposition the Commission was unwilling to risk its shaky reputation by advocating for women the same policy it required for blacks.

EEOC Chairman Roosevelt explained to Wirtz that while the Commission shared his concern about employment advertising, it had accepted

> recommendations of the newpaper publishers and classified advertising managers who proposed a means of avoiding unlawful expressions of preference while retaining traditional column headings. They requested an opportunity to make a good faith effort to comply.

The EEOC, Roosevelt said, would evaluate this "interim" policy at a later time.[30]

The inconsistency and questionable legality of the EEOC's ruling did not go unchallenged. In October Dr. Pauli Murray, a black professor of law at Yale University who had worked with the PCSW and had lobbied for the sex amendment to Title VII, delivered an angry public attack on the policy in a speech to a conference of women's organizations. Murray called the advertising policy a violation of the law. It was, she said, an example of resistance to equal job opportunities for women similar to the type of resistance used against blacks. And like blacks, women might have to march on Washington to secure equal opportunity for themselves. "If it becomes necessary," Murray said, "I hope women will not flinch from the thought."[31]

Murray's radical words were exceptional, but they reflected a growing anger among both officially appointed and self-professed spokesmen for women. Having discovered an antifemale bias in the poverty program, women's defenders saw an ominous pattern in the downplaying of the Women's Job Corps, the bunny jokes, and the new advertising policy. EEOC obviously felt little obligation to enforce those portions of its enabling legislation dealing with sex discrimination. Disregard for the statutory language made EEOC's policy an easy target for attack: it was clearly a violation of federal law. Yet an attack on the advertising policy would surely invite embarrassing comparisons to EEOC's slippery position on state protective laws which had been implemented at the request of the Department of Labor and supported by the Status of Women organizations. Railing against the EEOC's gradualism on classified ads while advocating caution regarding protective laws appeared inconsistent, and left women's leaders open to charges of indecisiveness.

Murray and Mary Eastwood, the Attorney General's ICSW deputy who opposed Keyserling's hard line on protective laws, attempted to clear some of the confusion and misapprehension in an article published in the December, 1965 *George Washington Law Review*.[32] "Jane Crow and the Law: Sex Discrimination and Title VII," drew on the recent work of state Commissions on the Status of Women to formulate a policy statement with a new point of view. The article's underlying assumption was that securing equal employment opportunity for women was just as important as securing it for black men. Murray and Eastwood did not merely accept Title VII's linkage of race and sex discrimination; they welcomed it. "The rights of women and the rights of Negroes," they argued, "are only different phases of the fundamental and indivisible issue of human rights."

Murray and Eastwood presented an alternative to the Women's Bureau's traditional stance on women's protective legislation. Rejecting, on legal grounds, the idea that these laws could be "harmonized" with Title VII, they predicted that the conflict between Title VII and state protective laws would be relatively short-lived. A review of state legislation likely to conflict with Title VII—laws restricting women from certain occupations, regulating the number of hours women could work, and setting weight-lifting limitations—convinced them that the number of women protected by these laws was small, and shrinking. While the laws themselves suffered from a "waning utility," the philosophy of protectionism was also losing its former appeal as equality of opportunity became a more compelling consideration. The report of the Tennessee Commission on the Status of Women, cited by Murray and Eastwood, gave the clearest indication of this shift in opinion:

> There was striking consensus among the Commission members against any semblance of protectionism. . . .Indeed, . . .the concern was the removal of inequities. . . .[T]here was equal concern that employed women recognize and pay the price that must be paid for equal recognition in the world of work.[33]

Murray and Eastwood applauded what they saw as a trend away from sex distinctions in labor legislation spurred by the state Commissions' efforts. "Relatively little harm would result," they said, if Title VII were interpreted to void most women's protective laws. Their argument was not unlike the position persistently defended by the "tennis shoe ladies" of the National Women's Party. But Murray and Eastwood, "insiders" to the Status of Women groups, fashioned the argument more compellingly. They showed support for their position within the state Commissions. And they drew upon the comparison of race and sex; "Jane Crow" was a new *persona*, more acceptble to women of the 1960s than the caricatured feminists of the 1920s.

Murray and Eastwood's article both reflected and encouraged the development of a recognizably feminist policy within the Status of Women groups. They presented a forceful and tightly reasoned argument for women to move beyond the WB's cautious protectionism toward an acceptance of equal employment opportunity for women as a legitimate, socially desirable, and important goal. Although many (perhaps most) members of the Status of Women groups continued to believe in the benefits of protective labor laws, the article helped clear the way for some to undertake an all-out defense of women's employment rights as guaranteed by Title VII.

Persuading the EEOC to strengthen its advertising policy was an immediate and unanimously supported goal of the Status of Women groups. They had an ally in Richard Graham, EEO Commissioner who served as Roosevelt's ICSW deputy. As chairman of an ICSW committee "to encourage a more positive climate of public opinion" for enforcement of Title VII's sex provision, Graham displayed a sincere commitment to women's economic advancement and won a reputation as women's friend at the EEOC.[34]

Graham's desire for a stronger policy on job advertising was actively opposed by EEOC Vice Chairman Luther Holcomb. A former Dallas clergyman with political ties to the President, Holcomb wanted to protect the EEOC from "going overboard" in defense of the sex provision. In December, 1965, Holcomb wrote presidential aide Marvin Watson that the American Newspaper Publishers Association (ANPA) was dissatisfied with the EEOC's advertising policy. Because he felt the EEOC's "big stick approach" was hurting the President's image, not only with the politically important publishers, but within the general business community as well, Holcomb offered to work with the ANPA in developing a less stringent policy. He asked that his work be kept secret to assure its effectiveness. President Johnson instructed Watson to have Holcomb report to aide Bill Moyers.[35]

No evidence of White House pressure on the EEOC remains in Johnson's files, but Holcomb was obviously not discouraged by anyone in the White House. By March, 1966, he was able to report success; he sent Watson a copy of an agreement he had worked out with ANPA representatives, satisfying all their objections. The agreement, which appeared word for word in EEOC's April 22 Guidelines, rescinded all conditions which the previous policy imposed on advertisements placed in sex-separate columns. While stating that advertising a sex preference for a job was illegal, the agreement gave companies covered by Title VII total freedom to use sex-segregated columns "to indicate that some occupations are considered more attractive to persons of one sex than the other."[36] (See Appendix B for April Guidelines.)

Learning that the EEOC had adopted an even weaker policy, Esther Peterson expressed her concern to Commissioner Graham, who told her that "pressure from the press" had been the key element in the policy change. Reporting this to Wirtz, Peterson commented, "any rationale for this action...is difficult to perceive." She anticipated strong reaction from groups interested in women's advancement, and added, "...there seems to be a possibility of court action."[37]

The strong reaction came first from Representative Martha Griffiths, whose efforts had been crucial to the sex amendment's inclusion in Title VII. In May, 1966, after the new policy appeared in the Federal Register, Griffiths sent a blistering letter to the EEOC, demanding an explanation of the "legal basis and policy justifications" for the new advertising guidelines. She also sent a copy of her letter to President Johnson with the notation, "I cannot believe that this is what equality of opportunity means."[38]

Holcomb, who became Acting Chairman of the EEOC in May when Roosevelt resigned to run for Governor of New York, answered Griffiths's letter. He argued that the EEOC did not regard advertising classified by sex as "completely analogous" with that classified by race. When employers placed job advertisements in racially separate columns, the purpose to exclude applicants of other races was clear. But an employer's decision to place advertisements in sex-segregated columns was, in the EEOC's view,

> generally based principally, if not entirely, on his desire to obtain a maximum reader reponse and not on a desire to exclude applicants of a particular sex....Thus it is primarily the reading habits of job seekers which presently dictate the placement of ads. Of course it should be noted that these column headings do not prevent persons of either sex from scanning...the page [for] jobs of particular interest to the individual....Nor do the headings indicate that qualified persons of either sex will not be considered on an equal basis for the advertised job.[39]

On June 20, Griffiths responsed by taking her case to the House of Representatives. Reading Holcomb's letter into the *Record*, she attacked his reasoning as "superficial" and "naive."[40]

> I have never entered a door labelled "men," and I doubt that Mr. Holcomb has frequently entered the women's room....The same principle operates in the job seeking process.

Griffiths's speech, which fills six pages of the *Record*, was motivated specifically by the new advertising policy, but it was also a protest against the "wholly negative attitude toward the sex provision of Title VII" displayed by "key officials" at the EEOC. At first, Griffiths said, she had excused the EEOC's negative attitude

> on the assumption that these men had not ever really thought about sex discrimination. Surely, I thought, when the evidence. . .began to pile up. . .they could not fail to see the close relationship between race discrimination and sex discrimination and to understand that race discrimination in employment would be only half eradicated if employment discrimination continued on the basis of sex. Surely, I thought, they would not ignore the fact that women's wages are much less than men's and that the poorest families in the nation are those headed by women.
> But their negative attitude has changed for the worse.

Public statements by EEOC officials seemed designed to cast "disrespect and ridicule" on the law. Griffiths was particularly incensed at a comment by Executive Director Herman Edelsberg that the sex provision was a "fluke. . .conceived out of wedlock." Although Edelsberg's characterization of the unusual circumstances surrounding the sex amendment's passage was close to the truth, Griffiths called it a "slur on Congress." She reprimanded him by asking,

> Since when is it permissible for an agency charged with. . enforcing a law to allude to the assumed motive of the author of legislation [Judge Smith] as an excuse for not enforcing the law?

Griffiths had no sympathy for the EEOC's lament that lack of a legislative history made it difficult to interpret the sex provision. Besides the debate on Title VII, she cited the lengthy legislative histories of the Equal Pay Act and proposals for an Equal Rights Amendment as germane to Congressional intent. But she reminded the EEOC that "such history is pertinent only where the statutory language is unclear."

The Commission's emphasis on problems in interpreting the sex provision served only to create further difficulties, Griffiths charged. As an example, she noted the efforts of several airlines to obtain a *bfoq* exemption for hiring flight attendants. Since airlines customarily hired both stewards and stewardesses to serve as flight attendants, Griffiths argued that sex could not be a qualification for the job. The problem would not have arisen, and the airlines

> would not be making such a ridiculous request if the EEOC had not been shilly-shallying and wringing its hands about the sex provision.

But the worst manifestation of the EEOC's negative attitude was the new advertising policy, which Griffiths called "the peak of contempt for women's rights." She rejected the notion that newspaper publishers' objections justified the new guidelines: "it is Congress, not the classified ad managers of the newspapers, that writes our Nation's laws." Her attack on the new guidelines made extensive use of the CAC's policy recommendations to the EEOC, and quoted also from Murray and Eastwood's article. But she went beyond discussion of the issues to question the commissioners' motives for their "flat hostility to the human rights of women."

> It is my firm belief that the EEOC's difficulties with interpretation and lack of legislative history are internal to the officials who wish the sex provision would go away....
> A little honest introspection, perhaps with professional assistance, would do more to help some of the EEOC staff than all the legislative history in the world.

Griffiths articulated the angry feelings of the emerging feminist movement, and helped focus them on the EEOC by placing the responsibility for enforcing a far-reaching and increasingly controversial law squarely on the Commission. She called upon the President to demonstrate his good faith by appointing, in the future, Commissioners who took all parts of the law seriously. She urged others "concerned with human rights" to join her protest, and suggested that "appropriate organizations" consider taking legal action against the EEOC. To encourage further action, she circulated copies of her speech to "several thousand women all over the country."[41]

Several persons close to the situation shared Griffiths's feeling that pressure from nongovernmental sources would be necessary to change the EEOC's attitudes. Commissioners Richard Graham and Aileen Hernandez, whose vantage point gave them particular insight, believed the EEOC would respond to organized pressure, and both privately urged women to consider collective action. Graham attempted to persuade the American Association of University Women, the League of Women Voters, and other national women's organizations to exert pressure on the EEOC. Betty Friedan later recalled Graham's telling her that leaders of these organizations were "appalled at the very suggestion," but she may have exaggerated their response. As early as January, 1966, AAUW and several other national groups were contemplating forming a coalition to work for equal employment opportunity for women; although the plans did not materialize, the coalition's prospectus indicates that elements of the Women's Bureau's traditional constituency were anxious for the government to take bolder steps on behalf of women workers.[42]

Pauli Murray, who suggested a women's march on Washington even before the EEOC relaxed its advertising policy, was also interested in organizing a women's pressure group. Her earlier speech attracted the notice of Betty Friedan, whose book, *The Feminine Mystique* had now become a best seller. While collecting material for a second book, Friedan met with Murray, and Murray began to introduce her to Washington's "feminist underground." This loose network of female employees in Congressional offices and executive agencies shared a frustration over the discrimination faced by women, and a strong desire to see Title VII effectively enforced.

Response to *The Feminine Mystique* led Friedan to believe that American women were ready to support a movement for change; talking to Washington's "feminist underground," she became convinced that a new kind of organization was needed to foment change, a group to fight for women as civil rights organizations had done for blacks. Existing women's organizations, with their stress on social welfare and community service, had shied away from self-interested feminist political involvement. The Status of Women groups were composed of executive appointees with numerous legal and political limits on their powers; the lack of a politically active constituency was a further check on their ability to make significant improvements in women's status.

The feminist underground Friedan met was, no doubt, a very small group, but its members understood the intricacies of Washington politics and had easy access to various sorts of information that would be valuable to a women's pressure group. These women did not, however, have the freedom to become politically active without jeopardizing their jobs. Friedan was under no such constraints, and her public identity as a champion of women's rights made her the obvious person to head an organizational effort.

The arguments of her new Washington friends, Friedan says, helped overcome her reluctance. Women with ties to the Status of Women groups are prominent among the list of Friedan's persuaders. Catherine East, a key figure in the feminist underground, was an employee of the Women's Bureau and Executive Secretary of the ICSW. (East found it expedient to keep her connections with Friedan secret.) Marguerite Rawalt, an IRS lawyer and former national president of the Business and Professional Women, had served on the PCSW and was a member of the CAC. Mary Eastwood represented the Justice Department on the ICSW. Pauli Murray had worked with the PCSW, as had Caroline Davis, Director of the Women's Division of the United Auto Workers (UAW). These women and others pressed Friedan to

> do what they knew had to be done and weren't free to do themselves. . . .to form a national organization of sufficient clout to get that law against sex discrimination enforced.[43]

Friedan agreed to try. Obtaining visitors' credentials as a writer, she attended the third national conference of state Commissions on the Status of Women in Washington in June, 1966.[44] She, Murray, and Dorothy Haener of the UAW agreed to seek out likely prospects among the delegates, and invite them to a meeting in her hotel room after the conference's evening session to discuss forming a new organization for women.

The timing was opportune. The state commissions had made sufficient progress to give them both a sense of confidence and a dawning recognition of the extent to which women's current status fell short of egalitarian ideals. Copies of Martha Griffiths's Congressional speech of the previous week distributed to the conferees insured that the policies of the EEOC would have a prominent place in conference discussion.[45] And dissatisfaction with administration efforts on behalf of women was intensified by the information, informally "leaked" by Washington's feminist underground, that the President did not intend to reappoint Richard Graham, whose term on the EEOC would expire in July.

The "maybe fifteen" women who met at Friedan's hotel room included Kathryn Clarenbach, Chairman of the Wisconsin Commission, whom Friedan invited after hearing her tell delegates they must "stop being afraid to rock the boat."[46] Friedan relates that her Washington friends were dismayed; they saw Clarenbach as "the darling of the Women's Bureau," and worried that she might somehow undermine their plans.[47] All the women present at the meeting were distressed by the EEOC's attitude. They decided to seek, the next day, conference resolutions supporting Graham's reappointment, and a more vigorous enforcement of Title VII's sex provision. But they turned down Friedan's proposal for a new organization as "too radical."[48] By noon of the following day, they had changed their minds.

The events which spurred this change, and precipitated the formation of an avowedly feminist pressure group occurred in a conference session called "Sex Discrimination—Progress in Legal Status."[49] The session followed the typical format: a series of official speakers addressed the delegates, who then divided into smaller "workshop" groups. Pauli Murray was one of the official speakers. She focused on the major concerns of the Status of Women groups during the past year, stressing the parallels between race and sex discrimination, noting the particular importance of Title VII to black women, lamenting the "attitude of derision" about sex discrimination, and charging that the EEOC's advertising policy "intimidates and discourages women at the very threshold of employment." Without mentioning the leaked news of Graham's termination, Murray noted that his term on the EEOC would expire shortly and urged the group to "express its interest in his reappointment."

Following Murray at the podium was Charles Duncan, EEOC's General Counsel, who contended that Title VII's sex provision had "awakened the national conscience" to the fact of sex discrimination in the workplace. Attitudes and practices, he asserted, were changing. Implying that greater change was possible, Duncan urged women to "put pressure on the EEOC to gain their ends." Unknowingly aligning himself with Friedan and the feminist underground, he noted that governmental agencies were accustomed to lobbying activity, and that the EEOC "welcomes and responds to such pressure."

Duncan's invitation may have caused Friedan's recruits to rethink their opposition to her proposal; the workshop sessions which followed clinched her argument that the Status of Women groups were incapable of the strong action that was needed. When one workshop, led by Marguerite Rawalt, tried to pass a resolution favoring Graham's reappointment, delegates were informed that the workshops were not authorized to pass resolutions.[50] The delegates could only talk; they were not permitted to recommend policy. The women who had been reluctant to act the night before were now "fighting mad."[51] At the conference's luncheon session, as Martha Griffiths and Esther Peterson addressed the delegates, Clarenbach, Friedan and others made plans to organize an independent women's pressure group.

Four months later, at its first formal meeting, the National Organization for Women (NOW) issued a "Statement of Purpose." In terms of the debate between equality and protection, NOW clearly sided against the protectionists; its statement announced opposition to

> all policies and practices—in church, state, college, factory, or office—which, *in the guise of protectiveness*, not only deny opportunities but also foster in women self-denigration, dependence, and evasion of responsibility, undermine their confidence in their own abilities, and foster contempt for women.[52] (emphasis added)

But the significance of the old debate was waning. The creation of a "civil rights organization for women" both reflected and contributed to a reformulation of the context in which federal policy for women would be discussed.

During the debate on the Civil Rights Act, when Judge Smith evoked laughter from the House of Representatives by drawing a parallel between race and sex discrimination, the defenders of women's interests were not amused. Further official joking about enforcing the Act's sex provisions aroused an angry unity among these women. The old divisions were not forgotten, but they became less important as increasing numbers of women began to view the race-sex parallel as both a serious matter and a valid basis for federal policy. The concluding chapter will examine the process by which sex was added to the executive order banning employment discrimination in government contract work, thus completing the parallel between race and sex in federal law.

Conclusion

Completing the Linkage, 1967 and Beyond

In 1963 the President's Commission on the Status of Women asserted that employment discrimination based on sex was so different from racially-based employment discrimination that separate remedies were preferable. President Johnson's affirmative action on female appointments obliquely suggested that similar remedies to these two problems might be pursued, but the sex amendment to Title VII of the Civil Rights Act of 1964 made the first and most important legal connection between race and sex discrimination. Judge Howard Smith introduced the amendment with jokes that "brought down the house."[1]

The amendment became law, but the jokes continued, arousing deep anger among the Status of Women groups and their allies in the federal government and national women's organizations. A series of negative experiences reinforced that anger. The Office of Economic Opportunity limited enrollment in the Women's Job Corps, failed to include women in its policy councils, and evidenced a commitment to Moynihan's strategy for ending poverty: taking opportunities away from women and giving them to men. The Equal Employment Opportunity Commission's weak guidelines and negative attitude suggested that this agency, like the OEO, considered sex discrimination a far less serious problem than race discrimination. This same reasoning spurred the PCSW recommendation for separate remedies, but the government's differential treatment of the two types of discrimination led PCSW's successors to reconsider the connections between race and sex.

The National Organization for Women accepted Smith's flippant parallel in earnest. Anger at the EEOC's failure to take the parallel seriously was the prime reason for NOW's founding. As a private organization, NOW operated under fewer restraints than the Status of Women groups, and its membership included many of the more outspoken and intensely committed of the women and men concerned with governmental policy on sex discrimination. But NOW had no monopoly on this concern; it was itself an outburst of the pressure steadily mounting within the Status of Women groups and among their allies. That pressure, given vital focus by NOW, was directed toward making the sex-race parallel an integral part of federal policy on equal employment opportunity. First, the legal bases of federal policy had to be brought into line with Title VII: the Executive Order requiring equal opportunity for minorities in federal employment and in work done under government contracts had to be extended to include women. Then, these laws had to be enforced, if not fully, then at least as stringently for women as they were for blacks. Securing parity with blacks in federal employment policy thus became the first political goal of the modern feminist movement.

Enforcement would obviously be a long-term goal, but the legal linkage between race and sex was completed quite rapidly. On October 13, 1967, just one year after NOW's organization, President Johnson signed Executive Order 11375. NOW is due much of the credit, but the federal Status of Women groups, which came to share NOW's goal, greatly facilitated this victory. Success, moreover, would not have been possible without a willing President. In 1967, as in early 1964, Johnson's political situation worked to women's advantage.

In September, 1965, President Johnson issued an Executive Order designed to reconcile governmental regulation of federal contractors' employment practices with Title VII's provisions. Legal complications, such as the question of Justice Department authority over companies which had filed affirmative action plans with the President's Committee on Equal Employment Opportunity, needed to be resolved, but political considerations were also involved.[2] Precedent suggested, and civil rights leaders expected, that contractors of government funds who discriminated in their hiring practices should be subject to stronger sanctions than were available for private employers. Executive Order 11246 provided such sanctions. It abolished the PCEEO and created an Office of Federal Contract Compliance in the Department of Labor to monitor government contractors' employment policies. The OFCC was authorized to suspend or cancel contracts with companies failing to comply with its regulations. PCEEO's oversight of employment practices within the federal government was given to the Civil Service Commission. The Order required both federal employers and companies receiving federal funds to establish affirmative action programs to recruit minority group employees. It also prohibited them from discriminating in any employment practice on the basis of race, creed, color, or national origin.

Sex was not included. It had not been among the types of discrimination prohibited by the PCEEO, and apparently no one argued for its inclusion in Executive Order 11246. The Status of Women groups appear to have given the idea no formal discussion, despite their opportunity for influence; Chairman Macy of the CSC and Secretary of Labor Wirtz, both ICSW members, were involved in planning the Order.

The questions raised by the Executive Order came at an awkward time for the CAC and ICSW. As early as February, 1964, after the sex amendment passed the House, but before it won Senate approval, CAC members discussed the amendment's possible application to government contractors. According to the official summary of the meeting, the members agreed that an executive order prohibiting sex discrimination by government contractors "would be helpful" if "introduced at the right time." Some members suggested having a recommendation available in case the President wanted to use it. Others opposed taking any action while the legislative situation remained so uncertain; their arguments prevailed.[3] At this same meeting the CAC debated its position on the sex amendment and concluded it was "too early" to decide.[4] In the summer of 1965, as the new Executive Order was finally being planned, it was apparently still too early for the Status of Women groups to formulate a position on the desirability of the sex-race parallel, although events were already pushing them to mitigate their concerns about protective labor legislation, and causing them to see the usefulness of the sex-race linkage.

Timing is important here. Executive Order 11246 was issued on September 24, 1965, after the White House Conference on Equal Employment Opportunity, and the *New York Times'* publication of the bunny joke. The Moynihan controversy was still brewing, and the CAC was preparing its policy paper for the EEOC. A change in attitude was clearly occurring, but it was still in its early stages. By October, after 11246's issuance, both the CAC and the ICSW had begun to discuss the desirability of encouraging further legal connections between remedies for sex and race discrimination. They recommended, after considerable discussion, that the model state fair employment practices law being drafted by the National Conference of Commissioners on Uniform State Laws include sex along with race and the other standard prohibited bases for discrimination. The CAC "strongly" suppported this recommendation, but the ICSW was reluctant to encourage the linkage.

Explaining the ICSW's hestiation to one of the Conference's consultants, Wirtz noted the same fears that had been expressed at the time of the sex amendment's passage: race and sex discrimination involved "different considerations," protective laws might be undermined, and "urgently needed measures...against racial discrimination" might be delayed or prevented if sex were added. The ICSW overcame its reluctance because a uniformity of state FEP laws could do no further harm to protective legislation; "it is clear, Wirtz said, "that a review of state protective laws for women will be set in motion by the Federal law [Title VII] in any case."[5]

This cautious approach suggests that the ICSW was simply not ready to grapple with the same issue as it applied to the federal government's own FEP regulations. It is also possible that the White House's delicate civil rights situation following the Moynihan controversy made anyone in the administration reluctant to complicate matters by raising the issue of sex.

Reluctance to discuss the possibility of sex's inclusion was not limited to the Status of Women groups. Curiously, no one seems to have paid much attention to sex's omission until after Executive Order 11246 was issued. An early hint of discontent surfaced in January, 1966, when several national women's groups, led by the American Association of University Women, discussed forming an organization to press for equal employment opportunity for women. Among their list of grievances was Executive Order 11246's omission of sex.[6] But the main focus of women's concern during late 1965 and early 1966 was the EEOC; not until summer, as complaints about its shortcomings mounted did 11246 begin to elicit public criticism.

Meanwhile, for reasons unrelated to the Executive Order, President Johnson turned his attention once again to women. The unintended outcome of this overture in early 1966, the amendment of 11246 to add sex, made it much more significant than Johnson's women-in-government campaign two years earlier, but this time Johnson was less enthusiastic, and less personally involved. The whole idea appears to have been forced upon him by aides and speechwriters completely unaware of the simmering criticism of the administration's record on women. They were seeking solutions to the more serious problem of the Vietnam War's effect on Johnson's political fortunes.

The occasion of Johnson's renewed "interest" was a ceremony honoring recipients of the Federal Women's Award, a recognition of outstanding achievement presented to six government career women annually since 1960. President Kennedy had always met with the recipients, as had Johnson, with seeming enthusiasm, in 1964 and 1965. But in 1966 he balked. John Macy and aide Jack Valenti urged him to reconsider. A Valenti memo, written three days before the scheduled ceremony indicates the nature of Johnson's political situation.

> This ceremony is the perfect stage for one solid blow of affirmation. . . .[I]t would ring out amidst the Vietnam clamor as one more proof of your deeper interests and this nation's basic commitments.[7]

Johnson agreed, and his speech writers began fashioning a "solid blow." They came up with the idea of a study group, composed of past Federal Women's Award recipients, to "probe deeply into the problems of working women." Noting that a recent traffic safety speech calling highway deaths "the greatest problem next to Vietnam" had received "great coverage," Johnson's writers added a "newspeg" sentence declaring the "underutilization of women...the most tragic and most senseless waste of this century."[8]

Johnson's speech of February 28, 1966, fell short of Valenti's anticipations. Just before delivering it, Johnson attended funeral services for the son of Merriman Smith, senior member of the White House press corps and an old friend. Smith's only son had been killed in Vietnam. Katie Louchheim, another Johnson friend, and Chairman of the Federal Women's Award board, reports that Johnson appeared gloomy at the ceremony, and read his speech in a monotone. She was not impressed by the content of the speech either; "some of us," she noted, "wondered about the need for another report" on women's employment problems.[9]

The Federal Women's Award Study Group on Careers for Women devoted its first year to studying careers for women in the executive branch of the government. One of the specific problems it addressed was prejudicial attitudes toward hiring, training, and promoting women within the government. In 1963 the PCSW's Committee on Federal Employment documented the existence of widespread prejudice against women in the executive branch; not surprisingly, the Study Group found that negative attitudes continued to limit women's advancement in 1966.

Reporting its findings to President Johnson in March, 1967, the Study Group praised his "active campaign" for improving the climate for women in the federal service but stressed that the persistence of discriminatory attitudes required "continuing counterbalancing pressures," more forceful than "existing regulations and directives." Since Title VII did not apply to federal employees, and Executive Order 11246 excluded sex, the Study Group recommended

issuance of a new Executive Order, or modification of the present Executive Order on Equal Employment Opportunity, to reinforce actions already taken to prevent discrimination because of sex.[10]

Johnson responded quickly and affirmatively to the report, releasing it to the press along with a comment that "clearly...something must be done." He approved all the Study Group's recommendations, and indicated that he would ask the ICSW to consider the "form of issuance" for the proposed Executive Order.[11]

During the year between the Study Group's formation and its report, sex's omission from Executive Order 11246 began to receive attention from women's organizations. A few groups sent resolutions to the President requesting a rectifying amendment: the District of Columbia Business and Professional Women in May, 1966; the National BPW in July; the Lucy Stone League in September.[12] In November the new National Organization for Women added its support.

Shortly after its founding NOW introduced itself to the federal government in a series of letters explaining its purpose and aims. A lengthy letter to President Johnson commended him for doing

> more than any previous president to focus national attention on the importance of bringing women into the mainstream of public and private employment

and pledged "active and continued support" for further efforts to insure equal opportunity. NOW's list of urgent needs reflected many of the concerns of the Status of Women groups; it gave top priority to straightening out the EEOC, and mentioned the need for a "comprehensive effort" to include women in the War on Poverty programs. Also on NOW's list was a request for Johnson to amend Executive Order 11246 by adding a prohibition of sex discrimination.[13]

NOW's officers quickly made their organization known to the federal bureaucracy. Although Johnson declined their request for a meeting, Justice Department officials and the EEO Commissioners met with NOW representatives, as did John Macy and Evelyn Harrison of the CSC.[14] Since Harrison was on the Executive Committee of the Federal Women's Award Study Group, NOW's list of demands was surely known to the Study Group, and may well have influenced its recommendation for an Executive Order.

The ICSW was particularly interested in NOW. In advance of its January 1967 meeting, ICSW Executive Secretary Catherine East sent each member copies of NOW's "Statement of Purpose," and its letters to the President, the EEOC, and the Attorney General. East, who was secretly involved with NOW, doubtlessly sought to focus attention on the new organization, but given the shared interests of both groups, such attention would be expected in any case.

At the ICSW meeting on January 17, John Macy reported on his meeting with NOW representatives, noting with apparent astonishment that they were not making the "kind of distinction which you and I have been making over the past five years," in giving sex discrimination "low priority in relation to other problems of discrimination." Wirtz responded that NOW was "a good thing to have in the picture" as long as its members could "also work someplace else."[15] Relations between the ICSW and NOW were strained, principally over the issue of protective laws, but remained cordial on the surface. The ICSW was genuinely supportive to NOW's concern about the EEOC's advertising guidelines; it agreed to send the EEOC a reiteration of its previous recommendations for stronger policy as a follow-up to NOW's appeals.[16]

NOW's existence prodded the Status of Women groups toward an acceptance of the sex-race parallel, and its recommendation for amendment to 11246 forced them to develop a position. An analysis prepared for Esther

Peterson early in 1967 favored an amendment adding sex. Another appraisal, possibly written by Catherine East, could find no reason

> why, after Congress included sex in Title VII, directing private employers to give women an even break with men, the Executive Branch gave its own contractors license to discriminate on the basis of sex.[17]

Peterson, and apparently Wirtz too, approved the idea of an amendment, and in February, the CAC endorsed it with a formal recommendation.[18]

Thus substantial support for amending 11246 already existed within the ICSW in March, when it received Johnson's instructions to consider the form of the order recommended by the Federal Women's Award Study Group. The Study Group's report dealt only with federal employment, and made no reference to employment by government contractors, which was also covered by 11246. It indicated that the ICSW should choose between an amendment adding sex to the federal employment section (Part I) of 11246 or issuance of a separate order forbidding sex discrimination in federal employment. John Macy favored a separate order, arguing that amendment of 11246 might be construed as "an admission of bungling in the original order." Macy's approval was important; as head of the CSC he would be responsible for enforcing whatever action was taken in regard to federal employment.[19]

Esther Peterson argued against a separate order, because, she wrote Wirtz, "sex discrimination should not be treated separate from other kinds of discrimination." She continued,

> I would also like to raise the related issue of sex discrimination by government contractors....Both the Citizens' Advisory Council and the NOW groups have recommended that...[all] parts be amended to include sex as a basis of discrimination. I support their recommendation and would suggest that the time is ripe for this step forward.[20]

Learning that the ICSW would be considering the subject, NOW sent an appeal to each ICSW member, urging amendment of 11246:

> [T]he excuses used by employers practicing sex-based discrimination are not substantially different from excuses regarding racial bias; and these excuses can best be met by the same law, agencies, investigators and government officials now experienced in combatting discrimination based upon race or religion.

A decision to create separate machinery for handling sex discrimination, NOW argued, would "in itself be a form of discrimination against American working women."[21]

Further important support came from the Federal Women's Award

Study Group. Just four days before the scheduled ICSW meeting, it notified Wirtz that having investigated the matter more fully, it now recommended amending 11246 by adding

> the word "sex" to the phrase "race, creed, color or national origin" wherever such phrase appears in the Executive Order.[22]

Because the Study Group appeared to have the President's full support, its recommendation, now in line with those of NOW, the CAC, and Esther Peterson, clinched the argument. At the April 18 ICSW meeting, John Macy acquiesced to the general agreement of "all whom he had consulted that sex should be included in Executive Order 11246."[23] The ICSW's recommendation went to President Johnson on June 2, and the Bureau of the Budget sent it to interested agencies for comment. Their agreement secured, Johnson signed Executive Order 11375 on October 13, 1967.[24]

Sending the order to President Johnson for his signature, aide Harry McPherson commented,

> women's organizations are said to be quite interested in this action. It is not really a major action, however, and should not be overplayed.[25]

Because most government contractors employed a sufficient number of workers to fall under Title VII's provisions (25 by 1968), even ardent supporters of 11375 could have agreed that its importance was more symbolic than substantive. The practical importance of 11375 was not recognized until 1969. Bernice Sandler, having been denied a job at the University of Maryland because she "came on too strong for a woman," discovered 11375 as a basis for individual and class action sex discrimination complaints against universities receiving federal funds. The spurt of complaints filed in the wake of her discovery gave important momentum to the feminist movement.[26]

But even the immediate importance of 11375 was greater than McPherson's remarks indicate. First, it completed the legal basis for a federal policy of equal employment opportunity for women. Along with Title VII and the Equal Pay Act, it not only provided the means to attack sex discrimination in employment, but also placed the weight of the law behind feminist arguments for equal employment opportunity. The respectability thus gained gave modern feminists an incalculable advantage.

Executive Order 11375 was also significant as an affirmation of Title VII's linkage of sex and race discrimination. Johnson implied support for the connection at the time of the Civil Rights Act's passage; with 11375 he bolstered its legal status, signifying that equal employment opportunity for women was not a "fluke," but a consciously undertaken federal policy. The

Order not only affirmed but completed the linkage between sex and race by making women part of all the government's equal employment opportunity regulations. Women had attained legal parity with blacks.

Securing enforcement parity with blacks was the next goal. From the start, the women's movement chose to focus on developing equal employment opportunities for all, rather than to admit it was competing with blacks for limited enforcement funds. The reality of that competition did not escape black leaders and civil rights supporters;[27] yet the movement's strategy would appear to have been helpful to blacks in the long term. By attracting a larger constituency, the women's movement eventually helped secure legislation broadening the EEOC's powers.

Yet another far-reaching effect of 11375 was its extension of affirmative action regulations to women. The concept of affirmative action, first developed for use by Vice President Johnson's PCEEO,[28] represented a momentous change in the theory of equal employment opportunity, and its application to women, who constituted a much larger portion of the labor force than blacks, tremendously amplified the impact of that change.

In the 1980s American society (not to mention the U.S. Supreme Court) is still unable to resolve the problems of affirmative action, for the concept is both a logical outgrowth and a contradiction of American egalitarian and democratic ideals. A brief review of changing American ideas on equal employment opportunity should help explain the paradox of affirmative action and also place the race-sex parallel in a broader context.

A general concept of equal opportunity has been a basic tenet of the American creed at least since the Jacksonian era. Never sharply defined, equality of opportunity at first connoted the individual's freedom to employ his talents and pursue his aspirations with the free play of economic forces serving as the only legitimate restraint. Although nineteenth century Americans would not have questioned the compatibility of liberty and equality, their concept of equal opportunity focused more on the liberty of individuals than on egalitarian ideals.

During the Progressive era—the time, not incidentally, when women's protective legislation was enacted—American opinion shifted toward a realization that liberty and equality were separate but interdependent. As a protection to equality, particularly equality of opportunity, society had an obligation to place certain limits on the free play of the market. These limits, determined by political means, would restrict the liberties of some citizens to protect and equalize the opportunities of others. The eventual enactment of laws placing restraints on freedom of contract by limiting hours and conditions of work were an outgrowth of the Progressive idea that government should serve as a referee to keep the play of the market fair as well as free.

The growth of the federal role during the New Deal years and the ideological and political effects of two wars fought in the name of democracy spurred further refinements in the political conception of equal opportunity. In the postwar years an increasingly potent civil rights movement called attention to inequities based on racial classification, and urged the government to assume responsibility for alleviating them. Arguing that racial discrimination was an impediment to the free play of the market, unfairly depriving a whole class of people from entering the competition, the early civil rights movement's view of equal opportunity focused on reforming the market process, the means to equality. Guarantees of equal employment opportunity—access to jobs on the basis of merit and without regard to such arbitrary classifications as race and religion—were particularly important in a society that defined a man by his occupation. State and federal Fair Employment Practices Commissions were outgrowths of this new consciousness, and Title VII of the Civil Rights Act of 1964 was its culmination.

The traditional view of equal opportunity necessarily implied unequal results, for it recognized the possibility of downward as well as upward mobility. Poverty, in this view, was the legitimate, if unfortunate, result of opportunity badly used. Equality lay in the process, not in the end result. This traditional view, with its emphasis on the freedoms of individuals, provided the basic philosophy for the civil rights movement. But that movement's success altered the traditional view by focusing attention on the disproportionate number of poor results experienced by black people in the competition for money, jobs, schooling, and other essentials of American life. Politicians and social planners, and of course blacks themselves, became increasingly conscious of the unequal results.

The trend toward emphasis on results was greatly accelerated by the cycle of poverty idea. If accident of birth could trap people in environmental circumstances which precluded their effective participation in the market, then poverty became not simply a result of inequality but one of its causes. Mere prohibition of discrimination was then an insufficient guarantee of equal opportunity. This realization led to the belief that government must be more than a referee insuring fair and free play; it should function as a coach for those unprepared for the game. This was the philosophy behind the War on Poverty, which, despite its imperfect realization, brought forth an outpouring of humanitarian sentiment from the American public, apparent evidence that the new view was acceptable.

President Johnson expressed this refined theory of equal opportunity most cogently in his Howard University address of June, 1965. "It is not enough," he said,

> just to open the gates of opportunity. All our citizens must have the ability to walk through those gates.

> This is the next and most profound state of the battle for civil rights. . . .We seek not just legal equity but human ability, not just equality as a right and a theory but equality as a fact and equality as a result. . . .
>
> To this end equal opportunity is essential but it is not enough, not enough.[29]

Johnson argued for what would later be called "compensatory justice," favorable unequal treatment to equalize, or at least minimize, the effects of past wrongs. He also gave political legitimacy to another departure from the traditional concept of equality: the idea that equal results were a legitimate *aim* of public policy. These ideas, implied in the term "affirmative action," further shifted the meaning of equal opportunity. The emphasis on individual liberty yielded to a more group-conscious, egalitarian view.

Although racial considerations were the basis of this change in American attitudes toward equal opportunity, the shift of focus from individuals to groups was readily adaptable to women. Like blacks, they were discriminated against as a group, on the basis of shared and highly visible physical characteristics. The economic status of both groups would benefit from legal prohibitions against discriminatory hiring practices, for both were excluded from society's most responsible and remunerative occupations. Women could also use the ideas of compensatory justice and equal results to their advantage if they were included among the favored groups. Title VII and Executive Order 11375 provided the legal basis for that inclusion, and the women's movement which developed in their wake secured the connection between race and sex discrimination by pressing for enforcement of these laws.

J. R. Pole notes in his thoughtful survey of *The Pursuit of Equality in American History* that as the idea of equality has been refined, the political dilemma has involved choosing not simply between equality and inequality, but rather among competing types of equality.[30] Such hard choices, reflecting the inherent tension between the individual/libertarian and group-based notions of equality, were not readily apparent in the expansive economy of the mid-1960s when the regnant optimism held that the economic pie could be made big enough for everyone to have a large slice. The conflict became more obvious in the next decade. Seemingly intractable economic problems combined with a new sense of environmental limitations to strain the notions of expansion and growth. Furthermore, the experience of devising and implementing affirmative action programs proved difficult. The use of equal results within selected groups as a test of equal opportunity was hard to distinguish from the use of a quota system, and quotas were incompatible with the ideas of individual liberty and free competition. Affirmative action goals posed the problem of competing types of equality in bald terms. Supreme Court rulings on several "reverse discrimination" cases cautiously upheld the constitutionality of affirmative action, but failed to resolve the question of how equality of results could be achieved while maintaining equality of opportunity as the means to that end.[31] The legal and ideological complexities of the problem, troublesome enough on their own, were compounded by the broad applicability of the potential solution. Because affirmative action applied to women as well as blacks and other minorities, solutions to "minority group" problems could potentially apply to a majority of the American population.

In 1963 Betty Friedan titled the first chapter of *The Feminine Mystique* "The Problem That Has No Name."[32] The parallel between race and sex discrimination, encouraged by the "NAACP for women" which she helped found, gave this problem a name: sexism. Applying the concept of racism to women's situation made it recognizable, and suggested a plan for resolving the problem. Women, technically a slight majority of the population, came to be seen as a minority group. The idea was not new: in 1944 Gunnar Myrdal had drawn the parallel, and other studies, such as Hacker's "Women as a Minority Group," (1951) developed it further.[33] But its acceptance as a basis for governmental employment policy, the process examined in this essay, was new, and had profound ramifications.

Racial issues gave the political landscape of the 1960s its characteristic shape. If the question of sex discrimination had been pursued as an issue entirely removed from this context, as the PCSW suggested, it was unlikely to become politically significant. In retrospect, it is hard to imagine how the sex-race parallel could have been avoided. While one might say that the "historical climate" was finally favorable to feminism's development, this author prefers Archibald Cox's explanation: "The idea of equality, once loosed, could not easily be cabined."[34] Ideas of equality borrowed from the civil rights movement began to diminish the distance between the stereotype and the reality of "women's place." Comparisons of women's situation with that of an oppressed minority opened a new approach, and a desire for women's equality replaced concern about women's status.

Emphasis on equality brought the demise of protectionism, both as a policy and a philosophy. State protective laws were undone, not by the EEOC, but by the courts. A series of decisions voided state protective laws on the basis of their conflict with Title VII. Feminist organizations composed largely of middle-class professional women provided funding and legal advice for many of the cases leading to these decisions, but a surprising number of the plaintiffs were the blue-collar (pink-collar?) workers whom the laws were designed to protect. By 1969 the EEOC revised its guidelines to reflect the decisions, and held that adherence to state protective laws would no longer be a defense for an "otherwise unlawful employment practice."[35]

Protectionism's downfall cleared the way for the Equal Rights Amendment. In 1970, Martha Griffiths pried it loose from the House Judiciary

Committee with a discharge petition, and serious debate began. In March, 1972, Congress approved the forty-nine-year-old proposal, and sent it to the states for ratification.[36]

Having rejected protectionism, women had only begun the process of defining their equality. The racial parallel suggested two possible approaches to equal employment opportunity. One regarded sex as totally irrelevant to participation in the labor force, and stressed equality of treatment for all workers. Another approach, based on the notion of compensatory justice, recognized the effects of past discrimination, and sought preferential treatment to bring women into the economic mainstream. But the sex-race parallel and the approaches it suggested had inherent limitations for women. Equal employment opportunity meant something different for them than for blacks, and the difference was connected with what the protectionists called "women's homemaking responsibilities." The concept of equal employment opportunity was devised as a means to advance the economic status of blacks, particularly black males. When applied to women it downplayed the social importance of their traditional nonmarket roles.

Equal employment opportunity for women could not be achieved simply by seeking equality with men in a society fashioned for male breadwinners and female homemakers. Protectionists responded to this fact by emphasizing the primacy of women's homemaking role and seeking, by statute, to make employers adjust their demands on women workers accordingly. The feminists of NOW advocated a different sort of adjustment, involving a relaxation of traditional sex roles and partnership marriages in which the breadwinning and homemaking tasks were shared. Yet restructured family roles offered, at best, only a partial solution to the problem of achieving equal employment opportunity. Changes in the structure of the workplace were also necessary, for it was still geared to workers with wives to provide supportive services. Patterns of advancement, for example, required intense devotion to career in the young adult years when couples most frequently become parents, and inflexible hours of work complicated the task of caring even for school-aged children. Because the rigid rules of the workplace had been made possible by women's unpaid labor in the home, their impartial application to both sexes did not result in a sex-neutral policy. Fully equal opportunity for women required structural changes in the workplace to accommodate women's needs and to facilitate the relaxation of sex roles.[37]

Feminists were slow to recognize the broad scope of this need, partly because it was masked by the race-sex parallel, and partly because their successful pursuit of a political definition for women's equality eventually aroused opposition, which forced them to spend energies consolidating their early and easily-won gains. This opposition arose from defenders of traditional sex roles, and focused chiefly on the ERA, which growing numbers of opponents saw as an assault on the laws of nature, a threat to women's "favored" position, and an unwarranted invasion of the federal government into the area of social mores. By the late 1970s, antifeminists had developed their own political networks, and managed to stall the move toward ERA ratification in the states. Feminist victories in attaining legal recognition of reproductive freedom for women also began to come under attack, as the relationship of women's reproductive capability to the general social welfare became a subject of heated political debate. Significantly, the bulk of support for both the anti-ERA and the antiabortion (or by their own politically astute term, pro-life) movements came from women. As women were drawn into the political process, the manner of policy making for women became increasingly democratized.

The beginnings of this democratization are clearly associated with Esther Peterson's orchestration of the President's Commission on the Status of Women. Peterson's skillful use of Kennedy's trust in her made the Commission an important event in women's political history. She later characterized it as a "step between Seneca Falls and Houston," (characteristically giving Eleanor Roosevelt credit for its success).[38] The PCSW, as Peterson intended, legitimized women's status as a subject for policy consideration, and began the necessary and tedious process of stimulating public discussion. In a "normal" political sequence, this might have led to definition of women's problems, proposal of legislative remedies for some of them, and public debate on those proposals. This was the sequence followed by the civil rights movement. But Peterson's carefully constructed PCSW, and the state counterparts it spawned, performed another significant function by creating what Jo Freeman calls a "cooptable network."[39]

The old debate between equality and protection moved toward a resolution as that network was "coopted" by advocates of the sex-race parallel. Riding the coattails of the civil rights movement, and benefitting from its legislative victories, these new feminists developed a vital concept of equality that undercut the protectionist philosophy. In the process, they added significant numbers of women to the policy making process.

These numbers decreased the likelihood that future decisions on women's policy would be affected by a woman in the right place at the right time. The method by which Esther Peterson secured the PCSW, by which Anna Rosenberg Hoffman prompted Johnson's appointment campaign, and by which Edith Green obtained a Women's Job Corps, is related to the "fluke" of sex's addition to Title VII: all are examples of haphazard, and intrinsically undemocratic policy making. Yet as long as women remained uninterested in the policy making process, the choice was between randomly made policy and none at all.

When feminists pushed their way into the policy making process, as they began to do with Executive Order 11375 and Congressional passage of the ERA, lack of opposition allowed them to influence policy with relative ease. With the development of politically significant opposition to feminism, the process has entered a new stage. The debate that failed to take place before the legislative victories—the debate about what it means, and ought to mean, to be a woman in America—is finally beginning to occur.

Appendix A

Major Female Appointments of President Johnson

Major appointments are defined as full-time jobs at level GS 17 or above. Only those appointments made by the President are included. The author has made every effort to make the list definitive, but due to the nature of White House record keeping, some appointments may have been overlooked.

The list was compiled from various sources, primarily: "Presidential Appointee Listing, Sort by Sex," Computer Generated Listings, and Presidential Appointee Directory, LBJL; Karen Keesling and Suzanne Cavanagh, "Women Presidential Appointees Serving or Having Served in Full-Time Positions Requiring Senate Confirmation, 1912–1977," Congressional Research Service, Library of Congress. Lists of past Women Chiefs of Mission, and Women in the Judiciary are found in "...*To Form a More Perfect Union*...," The Report of the National Commission on the Observance of International Women's Year (Washington, D.C., 1976), pp. 343; 347–48.

Key
*first woman to hold position
+appointee succeeded a woman
°new post

1964

*Virginia Mae Brown	Interstate Commerce Commissioner (Chairman, 1969)
*Mary Ingraham Bunting	Atomic Energy Commissioner
*Dorothy Jacobson	Assistant Secretary of Agriculture
*Mary Gardiner Jones	Federal Trade Commissioner
+Mary Dublin Keyserling	Director, Women's Bureau
*Elizabeth May	Board of Directors, Import-Export Bank
°Esther Peterson	Special Assistant to the President for Consumer Affairs

Charlotte Groshell Reese	Board of Parole, Department of Justice
Margaret Joy Tibbets	Ambassador to Norway
Katherine Elkus White	Ambassador to Denmark

1965

Eugenie Anderson	U.S. Representative to Trusteeship Council of U.N. with personal rank of Ambassador
Patricia Roberts Harris	Ambassador to Luxembourg (first black female ambassador)
°Aileen Hernandez	Equal Employment Opportunity Commissioner
*Penelope Thunberg	Tariff Commissioner

1966

+Eva B. Adams	Director of the Mint (reappointment)
*Carol Laise	Ambassador to Nepal
Constance Baker Motley	U.S. District Court, Southern District of New York (life term)

1967

°Genevieve Blatt	Assistant Director, Office of Economic Opportunity
+Betty Furness	Special Assistant to the President for Consumer Affairs
*Catherine B. Kelly	District of Columbia Court of Appeals
+Marian N. Rossmiller	Superintendent of the Denver Mint

1968

Joyce Hens Green	District of Columbia Superior Court
+June Lazenby Green	U.S. District Court, District of Columbia (life term)
Shirley Hufstedler	U.S. Court of Appeals, Ninth Circuit (life term)
+Elizabeth Kuck	Equal Employment Opportunity Commissioner
°Catherine Oettinger	Deputy Assistant Secretary of Health, Education and Welfare
*Margaret Price	Indian Claims Commissioner
*Alice Rivlin	Assistant Secretary of Health, Education and Welfare
*Barbara Watson	Administrator, Bureau of Security and Consular Affairs, Department of State

Appendix B

EEOC Guidelines on Classified Advertising

NOVEMBER, 1965

Help-wanted advertising may not indicate a preference based on sex unless sex is a bona fide occupational qualification for the job involved.

When a newspaper or other publication classifies such advertising in separate "Male," or "Female," and "Male and Female" columns, advertisers will most clearly avoid an indication of preference by using the "Male and Female" column. However, advertisers covered by the Civil Rights Act of 1964 may place advertisements for jobs open to both sexes in columns classified "Jobs of Interest—Male" or "Jobs of Interest—Female" provided (1) the advertisement specifically states that the job is open to males and females; and (2) substantially the following notice appears in a prominent place on every other page in the section in which the classified advertising appears:

NOTICE: Many listings in the "male" or "female" columns are not intended to exclude or discourage applications from persons of the other sex. Such listings may be used because some occupations are considered more attractive to persons of one sex than the other. Discrimination in employment because of sex is prohibited by the 1964 Federal Civil Rights Act with certain exceptions [and by the law of _____ State.] Employment agencies and employers covered by the Act must indicate in their advertisement whether or not the listed positions are available to both sexes.

APRIL, 1966

Help-wanted advertising may not indicate a preference based on sex unless a bona fide occupational qualification makes it lawful to specify male or female.

Advertisers covered by the Civil Rights Act of 1964 may place advertisements for jobs open to both sexes in columns classified by publishers under "male" or "female" headings to indicate that some occupations are considered more attractive to persons of one sex than the other. In such cases, the Commission will consider only the advertising of the covered employer and not the headings used by publishers.

Notes

Introduction

1. Jo Freeman, *The Politics of Women's Liberation* (New York, 1975), p. 148.

2. Frances Fox Piven, Panel discussion at conference, "Toward New Human Rights: The Social Policies of the Kennedy and Johnson Administrations," September 12, 1976, Austin, Texas.

3. Freeman, *Politics of Women's Liberation*, pp. 56–62; Sara Evans, *Personal Politics: The Roots of Women's Liberation in the Civil Rights Movement and the New Left* (New York, 1979).

Chapter 1

1. A copy of the Declaration and Resolutions may be found in Aileen S. Kraditor, ed., *Up From the Pedestal: Selected Writings in the History of American Feminism* (Chicago, 1968), pp. 183–88.

2. Robert H. Bremner, *From the Depths: The Discovery of Poverty in the United States* (New York, 1956), pp. 230–43; and Clark A. Chambers, *Seedtime of Reform: American Social Service and Social Action 1918–1933* (Minneapolis, 1963), pp. 61–83 give sympathetic accounts of the reformers' efforts.

3. 41 Stat. 987; 29 U.S.C. 11.

4. Eleanor Flexner, *Century of Struggle: The Woman's Rights Movement in the United States* (New York, 1972), p. 247; Mary Anderson, *Woman At Work: The Autobiography of Mary Anderson As Told to Mary N. Winslow* (Minneapolis, 1951), pp. 97–98.

5. The original version is cited in William H. Chafe, *The American Woman: Her Changing Social Economic and Political Role, 1920–1960* (New York, 1972), p. 112. Changes in the amendment's wording over the years did not substantially alter its content. The main clause of the version passed by Congress in 1972 states, "Equality of rights under the law shall not be denied or abridged by the United States or by any State on account of sex."

6. Judith Hole and Ellen Levine, *Rebirth of Feminism* (New York, 1973), p. 54.

7. Adkins v. Children's Hospital, 261 U.S. 525; Chambers, *Seedtime of Reform*, pp. 68–75.

8. Chafe, *The American Woman*, p. 127.

9. William O'Neill, *Eveyone Was Brave: A History of Feminism in America* (Chicago, 1971), p. 281.

10. Chafe, *The American Woman*, p. 123; Anderson, *Woman At Work*, pp. 160–61.

11. Quoted in Chafe, *The American Woman*, p. 123; see also Anderson, *Woman at Work*, pp. 160–61.

12. Chafe, *The American Woman*, p. 130; Anderson, *Woman at Work*, p. 172.

13. Anderson, *Woman at Work*, p. 160.

14. Chafe, *The American Woman*, p. 288, note 36.

15. Judith Sealander, "The Women's Bureau, 1920–1950: Federal Reaction to Female Wage Earning" (Ph.D. dissertation, Duke University, 1977), pp. 132–40; Anderson, *Woman at Work*, pp. 210–13.

16. Hole and Levine, *Rebirth of Feminism*, p. 55. Celler introduced Status of Women bills in 1948 and 1961.

17. Sealander, "The Women's Bureau," pp. 234–43.

18. United States Women's Bureau, typewritten pamphlet, "Action for Equal Pay," January, 1966, pp. 2–5, filed "Labor Standards," Reading File #16, Records of the Department of Labor, LBJL.

19. United States Women's Bureau, *Equal Pay Primer: Some Basic Questions*, Leaflet 20 (Washington, D.C., 1963), pp. 10–11.

20. Women's Bureau, "Action for Equal Pay," p. 5.

21. Ibid., p. 7.

22. Elizabeth F. Baker, *Technology and Woman's Work* (New York, 1964), pp. 411–21.

23. Leo Kanowitz, *Women and the Law: The Unfinished Revolution* (Albuquerque, N.M., 1969), p. 250, note 12.

24. United States Women's Bureau, *1969 Handbook on Women Workers* (Washington, D.C., 1969), pp. 10, 15.

25. O'Neill, *Everyone Was Brave*, pp. 232–49.

26. J. Stanley Lemons, *The Woman Citizen: Social Feminism in the 1920s* (Urbana, Ill., 1973), pp. 209–22.

27. William O'Neill, "Feminism as a Radical Ideology," in *Our American Sisters: Women in American Life and Thought*, ed. by Jean E. Friedman and William G. Shade (Boston, 1973), pp. 310–25.

28. Ibid., p. 301.

29. Carl N. Degler, "Charlotte Perkins Gilman on the Theory and Practice of Feminism," *American Quarterly*, Spring 1956, pp. 21–39.

30. Carl N. Degler, "Revolution Without Ideology: The Changing Place of Women in America," in *The Woman in America*, ed. by Robert J. Lifton (Boston, 1965), p. 204.

31. United States Women's Bureau, *1969 Handbook*, pp. 95–97.

32. United States Women's Bureau, "Fact Sheet on the Earnings Gap" (Washington, D.C., December 1971).

33. Valerie Kincade Oppenheimer, "Demographic Influence on Female Employment and the Status of Women," in *Changing Women in a Changing Society*, ed. by Joan Huber (Chicago, 1973), pp. 184–99.

34. Elizabeth Janeway, *Man's World, Woman's Place: A Study in Social Mythology* (New York, 1971), pp. 184–85.

35. William H. Chafe, "Looking Backward in Order to Look Forward: Women, Work, and Social Values in America," in *Women and the American Economy: A Look to the 1980s*, ed. by Juanita Kreps (Englewood Cliffs, N.J., 1976), p. 23.

36. Peggy Lamson, *Few Are Chosen: American Women in Political Life Today* (Boston, 1968), p. 78.

37. Cynthia Harrison, "A 'New Frontier' for Women: The Public Policy of the Kennedy Administration," *The Journal of American History* LXVII (December 1980), 635.

38. India Edwards claims that Truman contemplated naming Judge Florence Allen to the Supreme Court, until learning that the "Justices wouldn't have her." India Edwards, interview with author, Austin, Texas, November 10, 1975, p. 2. A transcript of the interview is on file in the Oral History collection at the Harry S. Truman Library, Independence, Missouri.

39. Karen Keesling and Suzanne Cavanagh, "Women Presidential Appointees Serving or Having Served in Full-Time Positions Requiring Senate Confirmation 1912–1977," (78–73G, March 23, 1978, Congressional Research Service, Library of Congress), pp. 18–35 lists appointees by administration.

40. Harrison, "New Frontier," p. 635.

41. Harrison, "New Frontier," p. 645.

Chapter 2

1. The conceptualization of Peterson's role and strategy used throughout this chapter is developed in Cynthia Harrison, "A 'New Frontier' for Women: The Public Policy of the Kennedy Administration," *The Journal of American History* LXVII (December 1980), 630–46. Earlier, and more lengthy, drafts of this article (generously supplied by Harrison, and in author's possession) are cited as Harrison Draft; in these citations, when applicable, Harrison's references are provided to facilitate corroboration.

2. Esther Peterson, interview with author, January 7, 1978, Washington, D.C. Hereafter cited as Peterson Interview.

3. National Manpower Council, *Womanpower* (New York, 1957).

4. Kirk H. Porter and Donald Bruce Johnson, comp., *National Party Platforms, 1840–1968* (Urbana, Illinois, 1970), p. 589.

5. Peterson Interview.

6. Ibid.

7. Ibid.

8. Harrison Draft.

9. News clipping, *New York Times*, March 14, 1961, filed with James Rowe to Lyndon B. Johnson, [March, 1961] Civil Rights, "Members," Vice Presidential Papers of Lyndon Baines Johnson, Lyndon Baines Johnson Library; Harrison, "New Frontier," p. 8; Eva Adams to John Kennedy, September 19, 1962, HU3, WHCF, John F. Kennedy Library, cited in Harrison Draft.

10. Harrison, "New Frontier," pp. 635–36.

11. Peterson Interview.

12. Ibid.

13. Letter, Esther Peterson to author, October 19, 1977, hereafter cited as Peterson Letter; Peterson interview. Peterson later forgave Johnson, saying she became very fond of Johnson's friend, Ellen Boddy; among the PCSW's experts and technicians, Peterson says, Boddy represented "the voice of the common person." Peterson Interview.

14. Harrison, "New Frontier," pp. 638–39; *American Women: The Report of the President's Commission on the Status of Women and Other Publications of the Commission*, ed. by Margaret Mead and Frances Bagley Kaplan (New York, 1965), pp. 255–65 lists Commission participants and their affiliations. Hereafter cited as *American Women*.

15. Peterson Interview.

16. India Edwards, interview with author, Austin, Texas, November 10, 1975. A transcript of this interview is on file in the Oral History collection at the Harry S. Truman Library, Independence, Missouri. See also India Edwards, *Pulling No Punches: Memoirs of a Woman in Politics* (New York, 1977), pp. 231–32.

17. Executive Order 10980, December 14, 1961, reprinted in *American Women*, p. 207.

18. Mary Eastwood, *Fighting Job Discrimination: Three Federal Approaches* (Washington, D.C., 1971), p. 29.

19. Cynthia Harrison, interview of Richard Lester, cited in Harrison Draft.

20. Reprint, Evelyn Harrison, "Facts Not Fancy About Women in the Federal Service," *Civil Service Journal*, October–December, 1963, filed "WB-CAC & ICSW" Reading File #24, Records of the Department of Labor, LBJL. Most civilian federal employees fall under the Classification Act General Schedule (GS) grades. The GS rank indicates the importance and the salary range of a job. The highest rank is GS-18.

21. Eastwood, *Fighting Job Discrimination*, p. 3.

22. J. Stanley Lemons, *The Woman Citizen: Social Feminism in the 1920s* (Urbana, Ill., 1973), p. 77; Mary Anderson, *Woman At Work: The Autobiography of Mary Anderson as Told to Mary N. Winslow* (Minneapolis, 1951), p. 153; United States Women's Bureau, "In the Federal Service: Equal Opportunity and Equal Pay," January 1965, filed "Labor Standards," RF #16, RDOL, LBJL.

23. Evelyn Harrison, "The Quiet Revolution," *Civil Service Journal*, October–December, 1962, p. 24.

24. "Memorandum on Equal Employment Opportunity for Women in the Federal Service," July 24, 1962, *Public Papers of the Presidents of the United States: John F. Kennedy, 1962* (Washington, D.C., 1963), p. 578; John W. Macy, Jr., *Public Service: The Human Side of Government* (New York, 1971), p. 84.

25. Donald R. Harvey, *The Civil Service Commission* (New York, 1970), p. 119.

26. Harrison, "New Frontier," p. 643.

27. Esther Peterson, "The Federal Equal Pay Law and Employment Equality," article submitted for the *Simmons Review*, filed with Peterson to Dorothy Williams, January 31, 1967, RF#20, "Equal Pay Bill, RDOL, LBJL.

28. Harrison, "New Frontier," p. 642; Harrison Draft.

29. Eleanor Stevens, "Some Developments in National Equal Wage and Employment Policy for Women with Emphasis on the Years 1962–1966" (Ph.D. dissertation, University of Illinois, 1967), pp. 63–64, 87.

30. United States Women's Bureau, *What About Women's Absenteeism and Labor Turnover?*, n.d., filed "Labor Standards," RF#16, RDOL, LBJL; Harrison, "New Frontier," p. 19; Stevens, "Some Developments...," p. 82.

31. Peterson Interview; Peterson Letter.

32. United States Congress, House Committee on Education and Labor, *Hearings on H.R. 898 and 10226, Equal Pay for Equal Work*, 87th Cong., 2d Sess., 1962; _____ *Equal Pay Act, Hearings on H.R. 3861 and Related Bills*, 88th Cong., 1st Sess., 1963.

33. Cynthia Harrison, interviews of Morag Simchak, Esther Peterson and Edith Green, cited in Harrison Draft.

34. "The Equal Pay Law: How It Will Work," *U.S. News & World Report*, June 24, 1963, p. 10.

35. See Thomas E. Murphy, "Female Wage Discrimination: A Study of the Equal Pay Act, 1963–1970," *University of Cincinnati Law Review* XXXIX (Fall 1970), 615–49, for a discussion of court interpretations, especially *Shultz* v. *Wheaton Glass Co.*

36. Peterson Interview; Judith Hole and Ellen Levine, *Rebirth of Feminism* (New York, 1973), p. 80; Willard Wirtz to John Macy, June 9, 1964, "Departmental," RF#4, RDOL, LBJL.

37. Caruthers Gholson Berger, "Equal Pay, Equal Employment Opportunity and Equal Enforcement of the Law for Women" *Valparaiso Law Review* V(Spring 1971), 331.

38. *American Women*, p. 32.

39. Cynthia Harrison, interview of Richard Lester, cited in Harrison Draft.

40. PCSW, Transcript of the Meeting of February 12, 1962, Washington, D.C., pp. 51–53 (Women's Bureau, Department of Labor), cited in "Harrison Draft."

41. *American Women*, pp. 64–65; Harrison, "New Frontier," p. 640.

42. Harrison, "New Frontier," p. 641.

43. *American Women*, p. 56.

44. Ibid., p. 74.

45. *Report of the Committee on Civil and Political Rights to the President's Commision on the Status of Women*, Edith Green, Chairman (Washington, D.C., 1963), pp. 27–28.

46. *American Women*, p. 48.

47. *Report of the Committee on Private Employment to the President's Commission on the Status of Women*, Richard Lester, Chairman (Washington, D.C., 1963), pp. 8, 15–18.

48. Ibid., p. 17.

49. Ibid., p. 7; Cynthia Harrison, interview of Richard Lester, cited in Harrison Draft.

50. Peterson, "The Federal Equal Pay Law."

51. *Philadelphia Bulletin*, November 24, 1963, cited in Martin Gruberg, *Women in American Politics* (Oshkosh, Wisconsin, 1968), p. 132.

52. Clayton Fritchey to John F. Kennedy, July 22, 1963, File HU3, WHCF, JFKL, cited in Harrison Draft.

53. Transcript of Interview with John F. Kennedy by Eleanor Roosevelt, for the *Prospects of Mankind* television program, released April 22, 1962, President's Office Files, Special Correspondence, Eleanor Roosevelt, JFKL, cited in Harrison Draft.

Chapter 3

1. Quoted in Katie Louchhein, *By the Political Sea* (New York, 1970), p. 183.

2. See James Sundquist, *Politics and Policy: The Eisenhower, Kennedy and Johnson Years* (Washington, D.C., 1968).

3. Daily Diary, December, 1963, LBJL; Lyndon Baines Johnson, *The Vantage Point: Perspectives of the Presidency, 1963–1969* (New York, 1971), pp. 29–31.

4. Born Anna Lederer in 1902 in Hungary, she came to the U.S. as a child. She married Julius Rosenberg in 1919, and was known as Anna Rosenberg throughout most of her public life. She married Paul Hoffman in 1963.

5. Caroline Bird, *Born Female: The High Cost of Keeping Women Down* (New York, 1971), pp. 90–91; Martin Gruberg, *Women in American Politics: An Assessment and Sourcebook* (Oshkosh, Wisc., 1968), p. 288, note 98; Eleanor Roosevelt and Lorena A. Hickok, *Ladies of Courage* (New York, 1954), pp. 203–4.

6. Transcript, Anna Rosenberg Hoffman Oral History Interview, pp. 2–3, LBJL.

7. Ibid., pp. 15–20.

8. Daily Diary, December 18, 1963; Memo, Juanita Roberts to Mr. O'Donnell, December 18, 1963, Appointment File, January 16, 1964, LBJL.

9. Daily Diary, January 16, 1964, LBJL

10. "Mrs. Hoffman at White House," *New York Times*, January 17, 1964, p. 17.

11. Liz Carpenter, interview with author, Austin, Texas, September 20, 1977. Hereafter cited as Carpenter Interview. See also Liz Carpenter, *Ruffles and Flourishes* (New York, 1970), pp. 28–29.

12. Carpenter Interview.

13. Letter, James Rowe to Lyndon Johnson, n.d. [3/61], Civil Rights, "Members" Folder, Vice Presidential Papers, LBJL.

14. *American Women: The Report of the President's Commission on the Status of Women and Other Publications of the Commission*, ed. by Margaret Mead and Frances Bagley Kaplan (New York, 1965), p. 74.

15. Gruberg, *Women in American Politics*, p. 15 and Jane S. Jaquette, "Introduction," in Jane S. Jaquette, ed., *Women in Politics* (New York, 1974), p. xx, both citing Harris poll data. For a more recent tabulation of women's voting patterns, see Marjorie Lansing, "The American Woman: Voter and Activist," in Jaquette, ed., *Women in Politics* (New York, 1974), p. 15.

16. Doris Kearns, *Lyndon Johnson and the American Dream* (New York, 1976), pp. 21–48; William C. Pool, Emmie Craddock, and David E. Conrad, *Lyndon Baines Johnson: The Formative Years* (San Marcos, Texas, 1965).

17. News clipping, "LBJ: Women Have the Courage," *New York Herald Tribune*, April 13, 1964, p. 14, filed "Utilization of Woman-power," RF #15, RDOL, LBJL.

18. Lady Bird Johnson, *A White House Diary* (New York, 1970), p. 54.

19. An exception was the luncheon of January 18, 1969, which singer Eartha Kitt used as a platform to attack the Vietnam War. See Johnson, *White House Diary*, pp. 682–88 for Mrs. Johnson's account of that highly publicized encounter.

20. Louchheim, *By the Political Sea*, p. 229.

21. Transcripts of Oral History Interviews for Goldschmidt, Rowe, Douglas and Hoffman, LBJL; Esther Peterson, interview with author, Washington, D.C., January 1, 1978. Hereafter cited as Peterson Interview. India Edwards, interview with author, Austin, Texas, November 10, 1975.

22. Elsie L. George, "The Women Appointees of the Roosevelt and Truman Administrations: A Study of their Impact and Effectiveness" (Ph.D. dissertation, The American University, 1972), p. 65.

23. "For the Cabinet Meeting," January 17, 1964, Appointment File, LBJL.

24. "Cabinet Hears a Woman Talk About—er, Women," *New York Times*, January 17, 1964, p. 12.

25. Carpenter Interview.

26. Appointment File, January 17, 1964, LBJL.

27. News clippings, Francis Lewine. "Status of Women to Get Johnson Lift," *Jacksonville* (Fla.) *Journal*, January 18, 1964; Bonnie Angelo, "President Seeking New Breakthrough for Women," *Syracuse Herald-Journal*, January 28, 1964, both filed "Utilization of Womanpower," RF#15, RDOL, LBJL.

28. Bonnie Angelo, "President Seeking New Breakthrough," Ibid.

29. News clipping, Marguerite Higgins, "Woman Hunt Is on Here," *Washington Star*, February 6, 1964, filed "Utilization of Womanpower," RF#15, RDOL, LBJL.

30. For the most recent, see *New York Times*, July 31, 1977, p. 1.

31. Isabelle Shelton, telephone interview with author from Washington, D.C., September 20, 1977. Hereafter cited as Shelton Telephone Interview.

32. Daily Diary, December 23, 1963, LBJL; Frank Cormier, *LBJ: The Way He Was* (Garden City, N.J., 1977), pp. 14–15.

33. Shelton Telephone Interview.

34. Memo, Liz [Carpenter] to the President, January 20, 1964, Appointment File, January 25, 1964, LBJL.

35. Daily Diary, January 25, 1964, LBJL; Shelton Telephone Interview; News clipping, Isabelle Shelton, "Johnson to Put 50 Women in Top Government Jobs," *Washington Evening Star*, January 29, 1964, p. 1, filed "Women's Bureau—CAC & ICSW," RF#24, RDOL, LBJL. Hereafter cited as Shelton Story.

36. Shelton Story.

37. News clipping, [AP], "LBJ Upgrading Women," *Washington Post*, p. B10, January 30, 1964, filed "Utilization of Woman-power," RF#15, RDOL. LBJL; "Johnson Seeks Women for High Federal Jobs," *New York Times*, January 30, 1964, p. 15.

38. Johnson, *Vantage Point*, p. 19; "The President's First News Conference, December 7, 1963," *Public Papers of the Presidents of the United States: Lyndon B. Johnson, 1963–64* (Washington, D.C., 1965), p. 35.

39. "Remarks Upon Presenting the First Eleanor Roosevelt Memorial Award to Judge Anna M. Kross, March 4, 1964," *Public Papers: Johnson, 1963–64*, p. 336.

40. Dean Mann and Jameson W. Doig, *The Assistant Secretaries: Problems and Processes of Appointment* (Washington, D.C., 1965), pp. 4–5.

41. Transcript, Mrs. Leslie Medgley [Betty Furness] Oral History Interview, LBJL.

42. Quoted in Gruberg, *Women in American Politics*, p. 285, note 73.

43. Many of these are filed Ex PE 2, WHCF, LBJL.

44. News clipping, Isabelle Shelton, "76 Women in Job Moves," *Washington Evening Star*, February 28, 1964, filed "Women" Folder, Civil Rights, Files of Fred Panzer, LBJL.

45. Explaining the committee to an associate, presidential assistant Jack Valenti wrote, "The idea is to use the committee to interest and reward nongovernment women who are community leaders." Memo, Jack Valenti to Bill Kilgarin, November 17, 1965, Gen FG 115/A-z, WHCF, LBJL.

46. Esther Peterson, interview with author, January 7, 1978, Washington, D.C.

47. Shelton, "76 Women in Job Moves."

48. The two were Mary Dublin Keyserling, Director of the Women's Bureau and Virginia Mae Brown, Interstate Commerce Commissioner. Transcript, Mary Dublin Keyserling Oral History Interview, LBJL; "Something for the Girls," *Newsweek*, March 16, 1964, p. 29.

49. Katherine Elkus White eventually went to Denmark; *Public Papers: Johnson, 1963–64*, p. 426. Margaret Joy Tibbets became Ambassador to Norway; Ibid., pp. 425–26; *New York Times*, July 10, 1964, p. 10.

50. Appointment File, March 4, 1964, LBJL. The author was unable to find any follow-up on this.

51. *Public Papers: Johnson, 1963–64*, pp. 232 (January 25), 339 (March 7), 425–27 (March 25).

52. Ibid., pp. 334–37 (March 4), 533–37 (April 24) 580–82 (April 28), 594–97 (April 30).

53. Ibid., pp. 460–61.

54. Ibid., p. 1194.

55. Ibid., p. 336.

56. Memo, Liz [Carpenter] to President, February 10, 1965, Ex PE 2, WHCF, LBJL.

57. Johnson declared "unconditional war on poverty" in his State of the Union Address on January 8, 1964, but it was not until March that his antipoverty legislation was ready for delivery to Congress. On May 22, at Ann Arbor, Michigan, he first outlined his goals for a "Great Society."

58. News clippings filed "Utilization of Womanpower," RF #15, RDOL, LBJL.

59. News clipping, Betty Beale, "LBJ Still Fighting for Us Women,"[Nashville] *Tennessean*, February 16, 1964, p. 15F, filed Ibid. Beale gave Johnson credit, but the policy of dissuading visiting dignitaries from speaking before the National Press Club was actually begun by Kennedy's State Department. (Information courtesy of Cynthia Harrison, personal correspondence with author.)

60. "LBJ's Hunt for Womanpower," *Saturday Evening Post*, June 27, 1964, pp. 86–87; "Ladies' Day; New Appointments," *Time*, March 13, 1964, pp. 22–23; "Something for the Girls," *Newsweek*, March 16, 1964, pp. 29–30; "More Women in Top Government Jobs," *U.S. News & World Report*, March 16, 1964, p. 19.

61. Memo, Esther Peterson to Liz Carpenter, November 29, 1963, filed with Lyndon B. Johnson to Margaret Hickie, January 1, 1964, Ex FG 686/A, WHCF, LBJL.

62. Memo, Esther Peterson to the President, January 20, 1964, Ex PE 2, WHCF, LBJL.

63. The bulk of this correspondence is in the four folders dated 11/23/63–4/30/64, Gen PE 2, WHCF, LBJL.

64. BPW Press Release, February 20, 1964, Chapel Hill, N.C., filed "Utilization of Woman-power," RF #15, RDOL, LBJL.

65. Memo, Esther Peterson to George Reedy, July 28, 1964, and Statement of Virginia Allen, presentation of "Accelerator Award," August 7, 1964, both filed with Lyndon B. Johnson to Virginia Allen, August 24, 1964, EX PP 13–14, WCHF, LBJL.

66. Conference on the Status of Women in the Federal Service, American Federation of Government Employees, "A Resolution of Commendation for President Lyndon B. Johnson," March 7, 1964, filed with Lyndon B. Johnson to Esther F. Johnson, March 30, 1964, Ex PE 2, WHCF, LBJL.

67. See above, note 63.

68. Memo, Evelyn Harrison to John W. Macy, Jr., November 25, 1964, RG 174, W. Willard Wirtz, 1964, "ICSW—(October–December)," National Archives; Civil Service Commission, Administrative History, Vol. I, part 1, chapter 3, pp. 50–59, LBJL.

69. Shelton Telephone Interview.

Chapter 4

1. United States Equal Employment Opportunity Commission, *Legislative History of Titles VII and XI of the Civil Rights Act of 1964* (Washington, D.C., n.d.), pp. 1–4, gives a concise history of federal FEP action. Hereafter cited as EEOC, *Legislative History*.

2. Transcript, Clarence Mitchell Oral History Interview, Tape I, pp. 24–26; Transcript Hobart Taylor Oral History Interview, p. 15; Transcript Burke Marshall Oral History Interview, pp. 13–15, Lyndon Baines Johnson Library.

3. EEOC, *Legislative History*, pp. 5–8; J.R. Pole, *The Pursuit of Equality in American History* (Berkeley, Calif., 1978), pp. 260–63.

4. See above, chapter 2.

5. *American Women: The Report of the President's Commission on the Status of Women and Other Publications of the Commission*, ed. by Margaret Mead and Frances Bagley Kaplan (New York, 1965), pp. 48–49.

6. Transcript, Mary Dublin Keyserling Oral History Interview, Tape 1, pp. 15–16, LBJL.

7. "Official Transcript of Proceedings, Secretary of Labor's Conference with Heads of State Labor Departments," March 17–18, 1966, "Labor Commissioners' Conference," RF#23, RDOL, LBJL.

8. Caroline Bird, *Born Female: The High Cost of Keeping Women Down* (New York, 1971), p. 12; Richard K. Berg, "Equal Employment Opportunity Under the Civil Rights Act of 1964," *Brooklyn Law Review* (December 1964), p. 79.

9. Benjamin Muse, *The American Negro Revolution: From Nonviolence to Black Power, 1963–1967* (Bloomington, Ind., 1968), pp. 82–84.

10. For a comparison of the original Kennedy proposal, the subcommittee revision, and the compromise House bill, see *Hearings on H.R. 7152 Before the Committee on Rules, House of Representatives*, 88th Cong., 2d Sess. (1964), pp. 360–61. Hereafter cited as Rules Committee, *Hearings*.

11. "Address Before a Joint Session of the Congress, November 27, 1963," *Public Papers of the Presidents of the United States: Lyndon B. Johnson, 1963–1964* (Washington, D.C., 1965), p. 9.

12. Lawrence O'Brien to the President, January 27, 1964, "Summary of Agency Reports on Legislation, H.R. 7152," Reports on Pending Legislation, LBJL.

13. Caruthers Gholson Berger, "Equal Pay, Equal Employment Opportunity and Equal Enforcement of the Law for Women," *Valparaiso University Law Review* V (1971), 332. Berger is a member of the NWP.

14. Rules Committee, *Hearings*, p. 125.

15. Ibid., pp. 366, 558.

16. Bird, *Born Female*, p. 3.

17. See Chapter 3. Johnson's and Smith's proposals developed independently, but the chronological coincidence is striking:
    Jan. 09 - Smith's first mention of sex amendment
    Jan. 17 - Peterson talks to Cabinet meeting
    Jan. 25 - Shelton interviews Johnson (50 jobs in 30 days)
    Jan. 26 - Smith on "Meet the Press"
    Jan. 29 - Shelton's interview published.

18. The author thanks Cynthia Harrison for pointing out the affinity between the NWP and the antilabor stance of Southern Democrats.

19. See, for example, Berger, "Equal Pay," p. 336.

20. Martha Griffiths, interview with author, Austin, Texas, November 11, 1975, hereafter cited as Griffiths Interview; Martha Griffiths, "Women and Legislation," in Mary Lou Thompson, ed., *Voices of the New Feminism* (Boston, 1970), pp. 112–13.

21. "The President's News Conference of February 1, 1964," *Public Papers: Johnson, 1963–1964*, p. 258.

22. Ibid., p. 259.

23. Stephen K. Bailey, *The New Congress* (New York, 1966), p. 81.

24. *Congressional Record*, 88th Cong., 2d Sess. (1964), CX, 1895–6; 2214–5; 2181–2; 2197–8. Two of the votes were by division: 43–115, and 26–112; the remainder were voice votes.

25. The only significant debate in the Senate concerned a "clarifying" amendment offered by Senator Bennett (R., Utah). *Congressional Record*, 88th Cong., 2d Sess. (1964), CX, 13168.

26. The February 8 debate on the sex amendment is recorded in *Congressional Record*, 88th Cong., 2d Sess. (1964), CX, 2484–92. References will not be given for each specific quotation; unless otherwise noted, all quoted material comes directly from the above-mentioned pages.

27. Bird, *Born Female*, p. 4., says Smith "brought down the house."

28. Esther Peterson, interview with author, Washington, D.C., January 5, 1978.

29. John Dowdy (D., Tex.) made the remarks.

30. Frieda Gehlen, "Women Members of Congress: A Distinctive Role," in Marrianne Githens and Jewel L. Presage, eds., *A Portrait of Marginality: The Political Behavior of American Women* (New York, 1977), p. 310.

31. Ibid. Gehlen's assertion is incorrect for at least one Representative; Elizabeth Kee (D., W.Va.) was not present that day. *Congressional Record*, 88th Cong. 2d Sess. (1964), CX, 2612.

32. In a teller vote, members favoring a measure walk in line past a "teller" who counts their votes; opponents then line up and are similarly counted. No names are recorded.

33. Final roll call vote on bill:
    290 (69%) pro
    <u>130</u> (31%) con
    420 (does not include paired votes)

    Vote on sex amendment:
    168 (56%) pro
    <u>130</u> (44%) con
    298

34. For an example of this intricate procedure's use, see Tom Wicker, *JFK and LBJ: The Influence of Personality Upon Politics* (Baltimore, 1969), pp. 109–16 .

35. Berger, "Equal Pay," p. 333.

36. Gehlen, "Women Members of Congress," p. 310.

37. Griffiths Interview.

38. *Congressional Record*, 88th Cong., 2d Sess., (1964), CX (February 10), 2707.

39. Herman Edelsberg, first Executive Director of the EEOC, quoted in Jo Freeman, *The Politics of Women's Liberation* (New York, 1975), p. 54.

40. *Congressional Record*, 88th Cong., 2d Sess., CX (Febraruy 10, 1964), 2613.

41. Ibid., pp. 2624–27.

42. Robert Griffin (R., Mich.) offered the amendment. The division vote rejecting it (15–96) is on p. 2634, Ibid.; Griffin's explanation of the amendment is on p. 2637.

43. Ibid., p. 2708.

44 Ibid., pp. 2708–09.

45. Citizens' Advisory Council on the Status of Women, "Summary of First Meeting, February 12–13, 1964," filed with Margaret Hickey to Members of the CACSW, March

20, 1964, "CACSW," Records of Secretary of Labor W. Wirtz, RG 174, National Archives Building.

46. Ibid., p. 4.

47. *Public Papers: Johnson, 1963–1964*, p. 328.

48. Bird, *Born Female*, p. 11.

49. Esther Peterson to Mrs. Cecil Norton Broy, March 27, 1964, and attachments, Gen HU 3, WHCF, LBJL.

50. Named after Senate leaders Everett Dirksen (R., Ill.) and Mike Mansfield (D., Mont.), the compromise was the work of many people, chiefly Senators and administration lobbyists.

51. Bird, *Born Female*, p. 11.

52. Griffiths Interview.

53. Lyndon B. Johnson to Modell Scruggs, April 23, 1964, Ex HU 3, WHCF, LBJL. Peterson prepared the draft for Johnson's signature.

54. *Public Papers: Johnson, 1963–1964*, p. 768.

55. The compromise did give the Attorney General power to bring suits where a "pattern or practice of discrimination" was alleged.

Chapter 5

1. Notable among these studies, because they found their way into the hands of President Kennedy, were John Kenneth Galbraith, *The Affluent Society* (Boston, 1958); Leon Keyserling, *Poverty and Deprivation in the United States* (Washington, D.C., 1962); Michael Harrington, *The Other America* (New York, 1962).

2. The term is Oscar Lewis's.

3. This statement greatly oversimplifies the complex, and often conflicting, ideas held by Americans about equal opportunity. In terms of classical political economy, for example, poverty is the legitimate, if unfortunate, *result* of *equal* opportunity. The development and implications of some of these conflicting views are discussed in the concluding chapter.

4. Executive Order 11126.

5. After replacing Esther Peterson as Director of the Women's Bureau, Mary Dublin Keyserling served as the ICSW's Executive Vice Chairman.

6. Administrative History of the Department of Labor, II, 240, Lyndon Baines Johnson Library. Reports of conferences at Marquette, Michigan (May 16, 1964); Duluth, Minnesota (July 17, 1964); Bismarck, North Dakota (July 17–18, 1964); and New Brunswick, New Jersey (October 17, 1964) are filed "State Commissions," Reading File #17, Records of the Department of Labor, LBJL.

7. Citizens' Advisory Council on the Status of Women, Summary of First Meeting, February 12–13, 1964, p. 6, filed with Hickey to Members of the CACSW, March 20, 1964, "CACSW," Records of Secretary of Labor W. Willard Wirtz, Record Group 174, National Archives.

8. [United States Women's Bureau], Summary of Proceedings of the [first] Conference of the Governors' Commissions on the Status of Women, June 12, 1964, "WB-CAC & IC," RF#24, RDOL, LBJL.

9. Interdepartmental Commission on the Status of Women, Notes for Secretary, January 17, 1967, p. 5, filed with ICSW, Summary of Sixth Meeting, January 17, 1967, "ICSW (Jan.)," WWW, RG 174, NA.

10. For Johnson's address, see *Public Papers of the Presidents of the United States: Lyndon B. Johnson, 1965* (Washington, D.C., 1966), II, 807–9. See also *Progress and Prospects*, A Report of the Second National Conference of Governors' Commissions on the Status of Women (Washington, D.C., 1965).

11. Members were the Secretaries of Agriculture, Commerce, Defense, Health, Education and Welfare, Labor, and State, the Attorney General, and the Chairman of the Civil Service Commission. A later amendment (Executive Order 11121, May 6, 1965) added the Directors of the Office of Economic Opportunity and the Chairman of the Equal Employment Opportunity Commission.

12. The original membership of seventeen was expanded with the 1965 amendment.

13. Transcript, Elizabeth Wickenden Goldschmidt Oral History Interview, p. 14, LBJL.

14. Esther Peterson, interview with author, Washington, D.C., January 5, 1978.

15. Peterson to Wirtz, January 6, 1965, "Miscellaneous," Supplemental File #A7, RDOL, LBJL.

16. The importance of Johnson's support may perhaps be gauged by comparison with later Presidents. Nixon appointed a CAC composed mainly of women to whom he or his party owed political favors. Lacking the representative character of the Kennedy-Johnson appointees, this group drew up a report which the Nixon administration considered too radical for publication. President Carter, too, experienced problems with his CAC, and caused a mild political flap when he fired its outspoken chairperson, Bella Abzug, replacing her with Johnson's daughter, Lynda Johnson Robb. Of course, the demands of the first CAC were quite modest, for neither a feminist view nor a feminist constituency had yet developed.

17. CACSW, Summary of Second Meeting, October 12–13, 1964, p. 25, filed with Hickey to Members of the CAC, February 24, 1965, "CAC," RF#25, RDOL, LBJL.

18. United States Women's Bureau, "Women in Poverty," July, 1964, filed "Poverty and Disadvantaged," RF#17, RDOL, LBJL.

19. CACSW, Summary of First Meeting, February 12–13, 1964, p. 9.

20. (Washington, D.C., 1964).

21. James Sundquist, "Origins of the War on Poverty," in Sundquist, ed., *On Fighting Poverty: Perspectives From Experience* (New York, 1969), p. 21.

22. *Public Papers of the Presidents: Johnson, 1963–1964*, I, 114.

23. Several participants in the poverty program's development have written accounts of the CEA-BOB and Shriver task force stages: John Bibby and Roger Davidson, *On Capitol Hill: Studies in the Legislative Process* (New York, 1967), pp. 223–38; Sar A. Levitan, *The Great Society's Poor Law: A New Approach to Poverty* (Baltimore, 1969), pp. 11–37; Sundquist, "Origins of the War on Poverty."

24. CEA, Administratively Confidential: Attack on Poverty, December 20, 1963, filed with Capron to Moyers, December 20, 1963, Ex WE 9, WHCF, LBJL. See also Robert Lampmann to Walter Heller, June 10, 1963, Administrative History of the Council of Economic Advisors, Vol. II, part IV, Documentary Supplement to Chapter V, LBJL.

25. CEA, Attack on Poverty, p. 5.

26. Ibid., p. 6.

27. Ibid., p. 8.

28. Ibid., p. 10-11.

29. *Hearings* before the Subcommittee on the War on Poverty Program of the Committee on Education and Labor, House of Representatives, 88th Congress, 2d session, on H.R. 10440 (Economic Opportunity Act of 1964), pp. 64-65. [Hereafter cited as *Poverty Hearings*.]

30. Ibid., pp. 114-115.

31. India Edwards, who sat in on some of the planning sessions, as Wirtz's advisor on youth employment, later described the Job Corps as a "total failure" because of this "numbers game." Interview with author, Austin, Texas, November 10, 1975, pp. 14-15.

32. *Poverty Hearings*, p. 192.

33. For further subcommittee testimony on the Women's Job Corps, see Ibid., pp. 368, 1525.

34. ICSW, Summary of Second Meeting, May 18, 1964, "WB-ICSW," RF#25, RDOL, LBJL; Wirtz to Green, May 21, 1964, "ICSW (May-September)," WWW, RG 174, NA.

35. Green to Wirtz, June 5, 1964, "Poverty and Disadvantaged," RF#17 RDOL, LBJL.

36. Jeanne Noble, "Ninety Days in Summer—Sixty Days in Autumn: A Report on the Work of the President's Task Force on the War Against Poverty, Women's Training Centers, Job Corps. June 1-November 15, 1964," EX FG 11-15-1, WHCF, LBJL. Hereafter cited as Noble Report.

37. Bibby and Davidson, *On Capitol Hill*, pp. 231-33, describes the personnel of Shriver's task force.

38. Filed "Poverty and Disadvantaged," RF#17, RDOL, LBJL.

39. President's Task Force on the War Against Poverty, "The Women's Job Corps—An Attack on Persistent Poverty: Working Paper," pp. 1, 8, July, 1964, "WB-CAC & ICSW," RF#24, RDOL, LBJL.

40. Ibid., p. 8.

41. Harold Bigler and Eugene Keith, "Helping Hands," *Manpower*, December, 1972, pp. 15-20; Transcript, Mary Dublin Keyserling Oral History Interview, Tape 2; Christopher Weeks, *Jobs Corps: Dollars and Droputs* (Boston, 1967), p. 182; Administrative History of the Office of Economic Opportunity, I, 540-41, LBJL.

42. Sar A. Levitan. "Job Corps," p. 29, "1968 Task Force on Job Corps," Files of Jim Gaither, LBJL.

43. Transcript, Mary Dublin Keyserling Oral History Interview, Tape 2.

44. Keyserling to Peterson, August 16, 1964, "Youth Corps," RF#27, RDOL, LBJL.

45. Keyserling to Wirtz, August 5, 1964, "ICSW (May-September)," WWW RG 174, NA.

46. Wirtz to Shriver, August 19, 1964, "ICSW (May-September)," WWW, RG 174, NA.

47. Shriver to Wirtz, August 21, 1964, "ICSW (May-September)," WWW, RG 174, NA.

48. Keyserling to Wirtz, August 20, 1964, "Miscellaneous," Wirtz' Office Files, Supplemental Files #A-7, RDOL, LBJL.

49. Edwards to President, August 20, 1964 is lost, probably somewhere in the caverns of the LBJL. A covering memo, Shriver to Moyers, September 1, 1964, Gen FG 11-15, WHCF, attests to its existence. Parts of the letter are quoted in News clipping, David Barnett, "Girls Urged in Job Corps," Washington *Star*, September 20, 1964, p. H-14, filed Gen HU 3, WHCF, LBJL. See also Edwards to President, November 9, 1964, Ex PP 2-2/FG 216, WHCF, LBJL.

50. Noble Report.

51. Bibby and Davidson, *On Capitol Hill*, p. 232, note 8.

52. Moynihan to Moyers, January 21, 1964, filed with Moyers to Jacobs, January 25, 1965, Gen HU 2-1, WHCF, LBJL.

53. Moynihan to the President, May 4, 1965, filed with Wirtz to the President, May 4, 1965, "White House—May, 1965" RF#9, RDOL, LBJL.

54. Ibid., p. 4.

55. Ibid., p. 5.

56. *Public Papers of the Presidents: Johnson, 1965*, II, 635-38. The quote is from p. 638.

57. (Washington, D.C., 1965).

58. Ibid., p. 29.

59. Pauli Murray protested censuring of black women for their "efforts to overcome a handicap not of their own making." Quoted in Lee Rainwater and William L. Yancey, *The Moynihan Report and the Politics of Controversy* (Cambridge, 1967), p. 185.

60. Moynihan to Harry McPherson, September 22, 1966, filed with McPherson to Cater, September 28, 1966, Ex WE, WHCF, LBJL.

61. Rainwater and Yancey, *The Moynihan Report*, gives a detailed account of the Moynihan controversy as it was viewed in its immediate aftermath. The authors relate women's concerns, but quite accurately, do not give them much emphasis in the overall story.

62. Significant Activity Report, November 15, 1965, RF#48, RDOL, LBJL.

63. Quoted in Rainwater and Yancey, *The Moynihan Report*, p. 186.

64. Griffiths to Wirtz, August 24, 1967, "ICSW (June-September)," Wirtz, 1967, RG 174 NA.

65. See, e.g., Angela Davis, "The Myth of the Black Matriarch," in Francine Klagsbrun, ed., *The First Ms. Reader* (New York, 1973), pp. 241-49; Pauli Murray, "The Liberation of Black Women," in Jean E. Friedman and William G. Shade, eds., *Our American Sisters: Women in American Life and Thought* (Boston, 1973), pp. 326-39; Cynthia F. Epstein, "Successful Black Professional Women," in Joan Huber, ed., *Changing Women in a Changing Society* (Chicago, 1973), pp. 150-73; Joyce A. Ladner, "Women in Poverty: Its Roots and Effects," in Anne F. Scott, ed., *What is Happening to American Women?* (Atlanta, Ga., [1970]), pp. 43-56.

66. Mary Dublin Keyserling quoting the director of a Washington, D.C. work-training program, Rainwater and Yancey, *The Moynihan Report*, p. 185.

Chapter 6

1. Kirk H. Porter and Donald Bruce Johnson, comps., *National Party Platforms, 1840-1968* (Urbana, Illinois, 1970), p. 589. The 1960 platform endorsed "legislation" to guarantee women equal rights rather than a constitutional amendment, but Peterson considered even that weakened plank a defeat.

2. *American Women: The Report of the President's Commission on the Status of Women and Other Publications of the Commission,* ed. by Margaret Mead and Frances Bagley Kaplan (New York, 1965), p. 66.

3. Restricted Item, Addendum to the Weekly Report, June 22, 1964, "Significant Activity Reports," RF#48, RDOL, LBJL.

4. Position Paper Assignments, unsigned, n.d. [June, 1964], Ex PL 5, WHCF; Wirtz to Moyers, "White House, July, 1964," RF#4, RDOL, LBJL; Porter and Johnson, *National Party Platforms,* p. 658.

5. Abernathy, et. al. to President, September 4, 1964, filed with Williams to Burke, September 25, 1964, Gen PL 1; Telegram, Elsie Hill to President, July 3, 1964, filed with Sinclair to Hill, October 1, 1964, Gen HU 3; Miller to President, August 29, 1964, filed with President to Miller, Ex PL 5, WHCF, LBJL.

6. Women's Bureau Division Chiefs Meeting, January 7, 1965, "State Labor Standards," RF#31, RDOL, LBJL.

7. Significant Activity Reports, March 8, April 5, 12, 19, 1965, "Significant Activity Reports," RF#48, RDOL, LBJL.

8. Keyserling to Wirtz, May 5, 1965, "Title VII," RF#17, RDOL, LBJL.

9. Wirtz to Roosevelt, August 9, 1965, "Departmental, August, 1965," RF#11, RDOL, LBJL.

10. United States Bureau of the Census, *Historical Statistics of the United States, Colonial Times to 1970* (Washington, D.C., 1975), pp. 127-28.

11. *New York Times,* July 21, 1965, p. 25.

12. Caroline Bird, *Born Female: The High Cost of Keeping Women Down* (New York, 1971), p. 13, the account followed by most later writers, attributes the joke to EEOC officials at the August White House Conference, but references to it in the report of the July conference of state Commissions on the Status of Women indicate an earlier origin.

13. *Progress and Prospects, A Report of the Second National Conference of Governors' Commissions on the Status of Women, July 28-30, 1965* (Washington, D.C., 1965), p. 40.

14. Ibid., p. 39.

15. Ibid., p. 42.

16. Ibid.

17. CAC members Marguerite Rawalt, Dorothy Height, and Ann Draper drafted the paper with help from Mary Eastwood and Mary Dublin Keyserling.

18. CAC, Draft Poisition Paper, September 10, 1965, notation on p. 14; Joseph Goldberg, Memo (for the record), September 23, 1965, "CACSW," RF#24, RDOL, LBJL.

19. [United States Equal Employment Opportunity Commission], "Report of Activities of the

First 100 Days of the EEOC," n.d., "EEOC," Files of Bill Moyers, LBJL. The conference met before the furor over the Moynihan report had subsided; Moynihan had resigned August 8. Although White House staff helped with the conference, the President did not take an active role.

20. *Report of the White House Conference on Equal Employment Opportunity, August 19-20, 1965* (Washington, D.C., 1965), p. 14, filed with LBJ to Roosevelt, January 6, 1966, Ex HU 2-1/MC, WHCF, LBJL.

21. Quoted in John Herbers, "For Instance Can She Pitch for the Mets?" *New York Times,* August 20, 1965, p. 1.

22. Ibid.

23. "De-Sexing the Job Market," *New York Times,* August 21, 1965, p. 20.

24. John Macy [Chairman, Civil Service Commission], *Public Service: the Human Side of Government* (New York, 1971), p. 92.

25. *New York Times,* p. 26.

26. CAC, "Equal Employment Opportunities for Women Under Title VII of the Civil Rights Act of 1964" September 27, 1965; Wirtz to Roosevelt, October 18, 1965, "ICSW (September–October)," Records of Secretary of Labor W. Willard Wirtz, Record Group 174, National Archives.

27. CAC, "Equal Employment Opportunities for Women Under Title VII," pp. 3–7.

28. Ibid., p. 8.

29. EEOC, Digest of Legal Interpretations, July 2, 1965 to October 8, 1965, in "Report of the First 100 Days," pp. 6–8. Announced in September, the policy was included in the EEOC's compilation of official Guidelines in November.

30. Roosevelt to Wirtz, November 2, 1965, "ICSW (November–December, 1965)," WWW, RG 174, NA.

31. Edith Evans Asbury, "Protest Proposed on Women's Jobs," *New York Times,* October 13, 1965, p. 32.

32. XXXIV, 232–56.

33. "Women in Tennessee, 1964," cited in Murray and Eastwood, "Jane Crow," p. 252.

34. Created at the October 1, 1965, meeting of the ICSW, Graham's committee eventually became the Committee on Mass Media. Peterson to Wirtz, January 7, 1965, "WB & ICSW"; "Current Appraisal of Issues Relating to the Status of Women," unsigned, undated, "Draft Papers on Title VII," RF#25, RDOL, LBJL.

35. Holcomb to Watson, December 16, 1965, Confidential File HU 2-1, WHCF, LBJL.

36. Holcomb to Watson, March 25, 1966, Ex FG 655, WHCF, LBJL. For further evidence of Holcomb's role, see Stanford Smith to President, May 9, 1966, with attachments, Ex PR 18, and Gene Robb to President, May 10, 1966, Gen FG 655, WHCF, LBJL.

37. Peterson to the Secretary [Wirtz], April 8, 1966, "Misc.," Supplemental Files #A-7, RDOL, LBJL.

38. Griffiths to Holcomb, and Griffiths to President, May 19, 1966, filed with Wilson to Griffiths, May 20, 1966, Gen HU 2, WHCF, LBJL.

39. Holcomb to Griffiths, June 1, 1966, reprinted in *Congressional Record*, 89th Cong., 2d Sess., CXII (June 20, 1966), 13055–56.

40. Ibid., pp. 13054–60. References will not be given for each specific quotation; unless otherwise noted, all quoted material comes directly from the above-mentioned pages.

41. Handwritten notation on a copy of Griffiths June 20 speech, "Equal Opportunity," RF#20, RDOL, LBJL.

42. Judith Hole and Ellen Levine, *Rebirth of Feminism* (New York, 1971), p. 82; Betty Friedan, *It Changed My Life: Writings on the Women's Movement* (New York, 1976), p. 80; Peterson to Schlei, January 26, 1966, "Women's Organizations," RF#30, RDOL, LBJL.

43. Friedan, *It Changed My Life*, pp. 80–81.

44. Ibid., p. 81; *Targets for Action, The Report of the Third National Conference of Commissions on the Status of Women, Washington, D.C., June 28–30, 1966* (Washington, D.C., 1967), p. 88. Hereafter cited as *Targets*.

45. "Some Activities of the ICSW Relating to Private Employment," unsigned, undated, "Draft Papers on Title VII," RF#25, RDOL, LBJL.

46. Friedan, *It Changed My Life*, p. 83; *Targets*, p. 41.

47. Friedan, *It Changed My Life*, p. 81.

48. Ibid., p. 82.

49. *Targets*, pp. 72–73 summarizes the speeches.

50. "Current Appraisal of Issues Relating to the Status of Women," p. 3.

51. Friedan, *It Changed My Life*, p. 83.

52. National Organization for Women, "Statment of Purpose (1966)," reprinted in Aileen S. Kraditor, *Up From the Pedestal: Selected Writings in the History of American Feminism* (Chicago, 1968), p. 369.

Conclusion

1. Caroline Bird, *Born Female: The High Cost of Keeping Women Down* (New York, 1971), p. 4.

2. Administrative History of the Civil Service Commission, Vol. I, Part 1, Chapter 4, pp. 6–8, LBJL.

3. Citizens' Advisory Council on the Status of Women, Summary of First Meeting, February 12–13, 1964, filed with Margaret Hickey to Members of the CAC, March 20, 1964, "CACSW," Records of Secretary of Labor W. Willard Wirtz, Record Group 174, National Archives.

4. Ibid.; see above, chapter 4.

5. Willard Wirtz to Norman Dorsen, November 12, 1965, with attachments, "ICSW (January-April, 1966)"; Norbert Schlei to Wirtz, November 4, 1965, with attachments, "ICSW (January-April, 1966)"; Schlei to Wirtz, October 29, 1965, "ICSW (September-October, 1965)"; Wirtz to Dorsen, August 27, 1965, with attachments, "ICSW (August, 1965)," all filed WWW, RG 174 NA.

6. Esther Peterson to Norbert Schlei, January 26, 1966, "Women's Organizations," Reading File #32, Records of the Department of Labor, Lyndon Baines Johnson Library.

7. Jack Valenti to President, February 25, 1966, Ex MA 1/F, WHCF, LBJL.

8. Charles [Maguire] to Jack [McNulty], February 26, 1966, Ex MA 1/F, WHCF, LBJL; "Remarks at the Sixth Annual Federal Women's Award Ceremony, February 28, 1966," *Public Papers of the Presidents of the United States: Lyndon B. Johnson, 1966* (Washington, D.C., 1967), I, 226–27.

9. Katie Louchheim, *By the Political Sea* (New York, 1970), pp. 184–86.

10. Federal Women's Award Study Group on Careers for Women, "Progress Report to the President," March 3, 1967, Ex MA 1/F*, WHCF, LBJL.

11. President to Penelope Thunberg, March 8, 1967, Name File, WHCF; Press release, "Federal Women's Award Study Group Reports to the President on Careers for Women," March 8, 1967, "Project Re-entry," RF#30, RDOL, LBJL.

12. Resolution of the District of Columbia Federation of Business and Professional Women... May 6–7, 1966, Gen HU 3; National Federation of BPW, "Resolution...July 28, 1966," filed with McPherson to Sara Jane Cunningham, September 28, 1966, Gen HU 3; Jane Grant to President, September 8, 1966, filed with Macy to McPherson, September 27, 1966, Ex HU 2-1, WHCF, LBJL.

13. Kathryn Clarenbach, et. al., to President, November 11, 1966, filed with Watson to Peterson, November 21, 1966, Gen HU 3, WHCF, LBJL.

14. Betty Friedan to Marvin Watson, December 5, 1966, with attachments, and Stephen Shulman to Watson, November 23, 1966, Gen HU 3, WHCF, LBJL.

15. Note from January 17, 1967 Meeting of the ICSW, "Draft Paper on Title VII," RF#25, RDOL, LBJL.

16. Interdepartmental Committee on the Status of Women, Summary of Sixth Meeting, January 17, 1967, "ICSW," WWW, RG 174, NA.

17. Carol Cox to Peterson, n.d., "ICSW (February, 1967)," WWW, RG 174, NA; unsigned, "Current Appraisal of Issues Relating to the Status of Women," n.d., "Draft Papers on Title VII," RF#25, RDOL, LBJL.

18. Peterson to Secretary [Wirtz], February 2, 1967, "CAC (February, 1967)"; Peterson to Secretary, February 8, 1967, "ICSW (February, 1967)," WWW, RG 174, NA.

19. ICSW, Notes for the Secretary, April 18, 1967, "ICSW (Meeting April 18, 1967)," WWW, RG 174, NA.

20. Ibid.; Peterson to Secretary, March 24, 1967, "ICSW (March, 1967)," WWW, RG 174, NA.

21. Clarenbach and Friedan to Wirtz, April 9, 1967, "ICSW (Metting April 18, 1967), WWW, RG 174, NA.

22. Penelope Thunberg to Willard Wirtz, April 14, 1967, "ICSW (Meeting April 18, 1967)," WWW, RG 174, NA.

23. ICSW, Summary of Seventh meeting, April 18, 1967, "ICSW (April-May, 1967)," WWW, RG 174, NA.

24. Agency assessments for Executive Order 11375 are filed with W.J. Hopkins to Secretary of Labor, October 16, 1967, Ex HU 2-1, WHCF, LBJL.

25. McPherson to President, October 12, 1967, filed with W.J. Hopkins to Secretary of Labor, October 16, 1967, Ex HU 2-1, WHCF, LBJL.

26. Jo Freeman, *The Politics of Women's Liberation* (New York, 1970), pp. 194–200.

27. See, for example, United States Commission on Civil Rights, *Jobs and Civil Rights: The Role of the Federal Government in Promoting Equal Opportunity in Employment and Training* (Washington, D.C., 1969), p. 55.

28. Hobart Taylor, who helped Johnson prepare Kennedy's executive order creating the PCEEO, coined the term "affirmative action." Hobart Taylor Oral History Interview, p. 12, LBJL.

29. "Commencement Address at Howard University: 'To Fulfill These Rights,' June 4, 1965," *Public Papers: Johnson, 1966*, II, 636.

30. J.R. Pole, *The Pursuit of Equality in American History* (Berkeley, 1978), pp. 248–58.

31. *Bakke* v. *Board of Regents, University of California* (1978); *Weber* v. *Kaiser Aluminum and Chemical Company and United Steelworkers of America* (1979); *Fullilove* v. *Klutznick* (1980).

32. Betty Friedan, *The Feminine Mystique* (New York, 1963), pp. 11–27.

33. Gunnar Myrdal, *An American Dilemma: The Negro Problem and Modern Democracy* (New York, 1944) pp. 1073–78.

34. Quoted (from another context) in Pole, *Pursuit of Equality*, p. 272.

35. Freeman, *Politics of Women's Liberation*, pp. 186–87.

36. Ibid., pp. 209–21 gives a detailed explanation of ERA's Congressional passage.

37. Mary C. Segars, "Equality, Public Policy and Relative Sex Differences," *Polity*, The Journal of the Northeastern Political Science Association XI (Spring, 1979), 319–39 suggests some of these changes.

38. Esther Peterson, interview with author, January 7, 1978, Washington, D.C. She refers to the first U.S. women's rights convention, held in Seneca Falls, New York in 1848, and the First National Women's Conference held in 1977 in Houston, Texas.

39. Freeman, *Politics of Women's Liberation*, pp. 63, 67.

Bibliography

Primary Sources

Collections at the Lyndon Baines Johnson Library, Austin, Texas:
  Aides' Files
  Administration Histories
  Appointments File
  Daily Diary
  Oral Histories
  Papers of Lyndon Baines Johnson as Vice President
  Records of the Department of Labor (microfilm)
  Reports on Pending Legislation
  Task Forces
  White House Central Files

Records of Secretary of Labor W. Willard Wirtz, 1963–1969.
  Record Group 1974. National Archives Building, Washington, D.C.

Interviews
  Carpenter, Liz. Austin, Texas, September 20, 1977
  Edwards, India. Austin, Texas, November 10, 1975
    (Transcript filed Oral History Collection, Harry S. Truman Library, Independence, Mo.)
  Griffiths, Martha. Austin, Texas, November 11, 1975
  Peterson, Esther. Washington, D.C., January 7, 1978
  _____. Telephone interview, from Washington, D.C., September 20, 1977
  Shelton, Isabelle. Telephone interview, from Washington, D.C., September 20, 1977

United States Government Publications

(Does not include published sources for which a location in the LBJL is cited in the footnotes.)

Bureau of the Census. *Historical Statistics of the United States, Colonial Times to 1970.*
  Washington, D.C.: Government Printing Office, 1975.
Congressional Record. 88th Cong., 2d Sess., 1964. CX.
Congressional Record. 89th Cong., 2d Sess., 1966. CXII.
Department of Labor. *The Negro Family: the Case for National Action.* [By Daniel Patrick
  Moynihan] Washington, D.C.: Government Printing Office, 1965.
Equal Employment Opportunity Commission. *Legislative History of Titles VII and XI of the
  Civil Rights Act of 1964.* Washington, D.C.: Government Printing Office, n.d.

Harrison, Evelyn. "Facts Not Fancy About Women in the Federal Service." *Civil Service Journal*, October–December, 1963.

――――. "The Quiet Revolution." *Civil Service Journal*, October–December, 1962.

Interdepartmental Committee on the Status of Women. *American Women, 1963–1968: Report.* Washington, D.C.: Government Printing Office, 1968.

――――. *Report on Progress in 1966 on the Status of Women.* Washington, D.C.: Government Printing Office, 1967.

Keesling, Karen, and Cavanagh, Suzanne. "Women Presidential Appointees Serving or Having Served in Full-Time Positions Requiring Senate Confirmation, 1912–1977," 78–73G, March 23, 1978. Congressional Research Service, Library of Congress, Washington, D.C.

National Commission on the Observance of International Women's Year. "...*To Form a More Perfect Union*...": *Report.* Washington, D.C.: Government Printing Office, 1976.

National Conference of Governors' Commissions on the Status of Women, Second, July 28–30, 1965. *Progress and Prospects: Report.* Washington, D.C.: Government Printing Office, 1966.

――――. Third, June 28–30, 1966. *Targets for Action: Report.* Washington, D.C.: Government Printing Office, 1967.

President's Commission on the Status of Women. *American Women: Report.* Washington, D.C.: Government Printing Office, 1963.

――――. Committee on Civil and Political Rights. *Report.* Washington, D.C.: Government Printing Office, 1963.

――――. Committee on Federal Employment Policies and Practices. *Report.* Washington, D.C.: Government Printing Office, 1963.

――――. Committee on Private Employment. *Report.* Washington, D.C.: Government Printing Office, 1963.

――――. Committee on Protective Labor Legislation. *Report.* Washington, D.C.: Government Printing Office, 1963.

President's Task Force on Manpower Conservation. *One-Third of a Nation.* Washington, D.C.: Government Printing Office, 1964.

Public Papers of the Presidents of the United States: John F. Kennedy, 1961–1963. 3 Volumes. Washington, D.C.: Government Printing Office, 1962–1964.

Public Papers of the Presidents of the United States: Lyndon B. Johnson, 1963–1969. 10 Volumes. Washington, D.C.: Government Printing Office, 1965–1970.

U.S. Congress. House Committee on Education and Labor. *Equal Pay Act: Hearings on H.R. 3861 and Related Bills.* 88th Cong., 1st Sess., 1963. Washington, D.C.: Government Printing Office, 1963.

――――. *Hearings before the Subcommittee on the War on Poverty Program on H.R. 10440, Economic Opportunity Act.* 2 volumes. 88th Cong., 2d Sess., 1964. Washington, D.C.: Government Printing Office, 1964.

――――. *Hearings on H.R. 898 and 10226, Equal Pay for Equal Work.* 87th Cong., 2d Sess., 1962. Washington, D.C.: Government Printing Office, 1962.

U.S. Congress. House. Committee on Rules. *Hearings on H.R. 7152.* 2 volumes. 88th Congress, 2d Sess., 1964. Washington, D.C.: Government Printing Office, 1964.

――――. *Hearings on House Resolution 789.* 88th Cong., 2d Sess., 1964. Washington, D.C.: Government Printing Office, 1964.

White House Conference on Equal Employment Opportunity, August 19–20, 1965. *Report.* Washington, D.C.: Government Printing Office, 1965.

Women's Bureau. *Equal Pay Primer: Some Basic Questions.* Leaflet No. 20. Washington, D.C., 1963.

――――. *"Fact Sheet on the Earnings Gap."* Washington, D.C., 1971.

――――. *1969 Handbook on Women Workers.* Bulletin No. 294. Washington, D.C.: Government Printing Office, 1969.

Secondary Sources

Anderson, Mary. *Women at Work: The Autobiography of Mary Anderson as Told to Mary N. Winslow*. Minneapolis: University of Minnesota Press, 1951.

Bailey, Stephen K. *The New Congress*. New York: St. Martin's Press, 1966.

Baker, Elizabeth F. *Technology and Women's Work*. New York: Columbia University Press, 1964.

Berg, Richard K. "Equal Employment Opportunity under the Civil Rights Act of 1964." *Brooklyn Law Review*, December 1964 pp. 62–97.

Berger, Caruthers Gholson. "Equal Pay, Equal Employment Opportunity and Equal Enforcement of the Law for Women." *Valparaiso Law Review* V (Spring, 1971), 326–73.

Bibby, John, and Davidson, Roger. *On Capitol Hill: Studies in the Legislative Process*. New York: Holt, Rinehart & Winston, 1967.

Bigler, Harold, and Keith, Eugene. "Helping Hands." *Manpower*, December 1972, pp. 15–20.

Bird, Caroline. *Born Female: The High Cost of Keeping Women Down*. Revised edition. New York: Pocket Books, 1971.

Bremner, Rober H. *From the Depths: The Discovery of Poverty in the United States*. New York: New York University Press, 1956.

Carpenter, Liz. *Ruffles and Flourishes*. New York: Doubleday, 1970.

Chafe, William H. *The American Woman: Her Changing Social, Economic and Political Role, 1920–1970*. New York: Oxford University Press, 1972.

———. "Looking Backward in Order to Look Forward: Women, Work, and Social Values in America." In *Women and the American Economy*, edited by Juanita M. Kreps. Englewood Cliffs, N.J.: Prentice-Hall, 1976.

Chambers, Clark A. *Seedtime of Reform: American Social Service and Social Action, 1918–1933*. Minneapolis: University of Minnesota Press, 1963.

Cormier, Frank. *LBJ: The Way He Was*. Garden City, N.J.: Doubleday, 1977.

Curtoys, Charles Jeremy. "The Paradox of Equality: A Study of the California Fair Employment Practice Commission." Ph.D. dissertation, University of California, Berkeley, 1976. .

Davis, Angela. "The Myth of the Black Matriarch." In *The First Ms. Reader*, edited by Francine Klagsbrun. New York: Warner Paperbacks, 1973.

Degler, Carl N. "Charlotte Perkins Gilman on the Theory and Practice of Feminism." *American Quarterly*, Spring 1956, pp. 21–39.

———. "Revolution Without Ideology: The Changing Place of Women in America." In *The Woman in America* edited by Robert J. Lifton. Boston: Houghton Mifflin, 1965.

Eastwood, Mary. *Fighting Job Discrimination: Three Federal Approches*. Washington, D. C.: Today Publications and News Service, 1971.

Edwards, India. *Pulling No Punches: Memoirs of a Woman in Politics*. New York: Putnam, 1977.

Epstein, Cynthia Fuchs. "Successful Black Professional Women." In *Changing Women in a Changing Society*, edited by Joan Huber. Chicago: University of Chicago Press, 1973.

Evans, Sara. *Personal Politics: The Roots of Women's Liberation in the Civil Rights Movement and the New Left*. New York: Knopf, 1979.

Flexner, Eleanor. *Century of Struggle: The Woman's Rights Movement in the United States*. New York: Atheneum, 1972.

Freeman, Jo. *The Politics of Women's Liberation: A Case Study of an Emerging Social Movement and its Relation to the Policy Process*. New York: David McKay, 1975.

Friedan, Betty. *The Feminine Mystique*. New York: W.W. Norton, 1963.

———. *It Changed My Life: Writings on the Women's Movement*. New York: Random House, 1976.

Galbraith, John Kenneth. *The Affluent Society*. Boston: Houghton-Mifflin, 1958.

Gehlen, Frieda. "Women Members of Congress: A Distinctive Role." In *A Portrait of Marginality: The Political Behavior of the American Woman*, edited by Marianne Githens and Jewel L. Presage. New York: David McKay, 1977.

George, Elsie L. "The Women Appointees of the Roosevelt and Truman Administrations: A Study of Their Impact and Effectiveness." Ph.D. dissertation, The American University, 1972.

Griffiths, Martha. "Women and Legislation." In *Voices of the New Feminism*, edited by Mary Lou Thompson. Boston: Beacon Press, 1970.

Gruberg, Martin. *Women in American Politics: An Assessment and Sourcebook*. Oshkosh, Wisconsin: Academia Press, 1968.

Hacker, Helen Mayer. "Women as a Minority Group." *Social Forces*, October 1951, pp. 60–69.

Harrington, Michael. *The Other America*. New York: Macmillan, 1962.

Harrison, Cynthia. "A 'New Frontier' for Women: The Public Policy of the Kennedy Administration." *The Journal of American History* LXVII (December 1980), 630–46.

Harvey, Donald R. *The Civil Service Commission*. New York: Praeger, 1970.

Hole, Judith, and Levine, Ellen. *Rebirth of Feminism*. New York: Quadrangle, 1971.

Janeway, Elizabeth. *Man's World, Woman's Place: A Study in Social Mythology*. New York: Delta, 1971.

Jaquette, Jane S. "Introduction." In *Women in Politics*, edited by Jane S. Jaquette. New York: John Wiley & Sons, 1974.

Johnson, Lady Bird. *A White House Diary*. New York: Holt, Rinehart and Winston, 1970.

Johnson, Lyndon Baines. *The Vantage Point: Perspectives of the Presidency, 1963–1969*. New York: Holt, Rinehart and Winston, 1971.

Kanowitz, Leo. *Women and the Law: The Unfinished Revolution*. Albuquerque: University of New Mexico Press, 1969.

Kearns, Doris. *Lyndon Johnson and the American Dream*. New York: Harper and Row, 1976.

Keyserling, Leon. *Poverty and Deprivation in the United States*. Washington, D.C.: Conference on Economic Progress, 1962.

Kraditor, Aileen S., ed. *Up From the Pedestal: Selected Writings in the History of American Feminism*. Chicago: Quadrangle, 1968.

Ladner, Joyce A. "Women in Poverty: Its Roots and Effects." In *What Is Happening to American Women?*, edited by Anne Firor Scott. Atlanta, Georgia: Southern Newspaper Publishers Association, n.d. [1970].

Lamson, Peggy. *Few Are Chosen: American Women in Political Life Today*. Boston: Houghton-Mifflin, 1968.

Lansing, Marjorie. "The American Woman: Voter and Activist." In *Women in Politics*, edited by Jane S. Jaquette. New York: John Wiley & Sons, 1974.

Lemons, J. Stanley. *The Woman Citizen: Social Feminism in the 1920s*. Urbana: University of Illinois Press, 1973.

Levitan, Sar. *The Great Society's Poor Law: A New Approach to Poverty*. Baltimore: Johns Hopkins Press, 1969.

Lisagor, Peter, and Higgins, Marguerite. "LBJ's Hunt for Womanpower." *Saturday Evening Post*, June 27, 1964.

Louchheim, Katie. *By the Political Sea*. New York: Doubleday, 1970.

Macy, John W., Jr. *Public Service: The Human Side of Government*. New York: Harper and Row, 1971.

Mann, Dean, and Doig, Jameson W. *The Assistant Secretaries: Problems and Processes of Appointment*. Washington, D.C.: The Brookings Institution, 1965.

Murphy, Thomas E. "Female Wage Discrimination: A Study of the Equal Pay Act, 1963–1970." *University of Cincinnati Law Review* XXXIX (Fall 1970), 615–49.

Murray, Pauli. "The Liberation of Black Women." In *Our American Sisters: Women in American Life and Thought*, edited by Jean E. Friedman and William G. Shade. Boston: Allyn and Bacon, 1973.

———, and Eastwood, Mary. "Jane Crow and the Law: Sex Discrimination and Title VII." *George Washington Law Review* XXXIV (December 1965), 232–56.

Muse, Benjamin. *The American Negro Revolution: From Nonviolence to Black Power, 1963–1967*. Bloomington: Indiana University Press, 1968.

Myrdal, Gunnar. *An American Dilemma: The Negro Problem and Modern Democracy*. New York: Harper & Brothers, 1944.

National Manpower Council. *Womanpower*. New York: Columbia University Press, 1957.

New York Times
  January 17, 1964, pp. 12, 17
  January 30, 1964, p. 15
  July 10, 1964, p. 10
  July 21, 1965, p. 25
  August 20, 1965 p. 1
  August 21, 1965, p. 20
  October 13, 1965, p. 32
  July 31, 1977, p. 1

Newsweek. "Something for the Girls." March 16, 1964, pp. 29–30.

Nye, Ivan F., and Hoffman, Lois W. "The Socio-Cultural Setting." In *The Other Half: Roads to Women's Equility*, edited by Cynthia F. Epstein and William J. Goode. Englewood Cliffs, New Jersey: Prentice-Hall, 1971.

O'Neill, William. *Eveyone Was Brave: A History of Feminism in America*. New York: Times Books, 1972.

———. "Feminism as a Radical Ideology." In *Our American Sisters: Women in American Life and Thought*, edited by Jean E. Friedman and William G. Shade. Boston: Allyn and Bacon, 1973.

Oppenheimer, Valerie Kincade. "Demographic Influence on Female Employment and the Status of Women." In *Changing Women in a Changing Society*, edited by Joan Huber. Chicago: University of Chicago Press, 1973.

Pole, J.R. *The Pursuit of Equality in American History*. Berkeley: University of California Press, 1978.

Pool, William C., Craddock, Emmie, and Conrad, David E. *Lyndon Baines Johnson: The Formative Years*. San Marcos, Texas: Southwest State College Press, 1965.

Porter, Kirk H., and Johnson, Donald Bruce, comps. *National Party Platforms, 1840–1968*. Urbana: University of Illinois Press, 1970.

President's Commission on the Status of Women. *American Women: Report. . .and Other Publications of the Commission*. Edited by Margaret Mead and Francis Bagley Kaplan. New York: Charles Scribner's Sons, 1965.

Rainwater, Lee, and Yancey, William L. *The Moynihan Report and the Politics of Controversy*. Cambridge, Massachusetts: The M.I.T. Press, 1967.

Roosevelt, Eleanor, and Hickok, Lorena A. *Ladies of Courage*. New York: G.P. Putnam's Sons, 1954.

Sealander, Judith. "The Women's Bureau, 1920–1950: Federal Reaction to Female Wage Earning." Ph.D. dissertation, Duke University, 1977.

Segars, Mary C. "Equality, Public Policy and Relative Sex Differences." *Polity, The Journal of the Northeastern Political Science Association* XI (Spring 1979), 319–39.

Stevens, Eleanor. "Some Developments in National Wage and Employment Policy for Women with Emphasis on the Years 1962–1966." Ph.D. dissertation, University of Illinois, 1967.

Sundquist, James. "Origins of the War on Poverty." In *On Fighting Poverty*, edited by James Sundquist. New York: Basic Books, 1969.

_____. *Politics and Policy: The Eisenhower, Kennedy and Johnson Years*. Washington, D.C.: The Brookings Institution, 1968.

Time. "Ladies' Day; New Appointments." March 13, 1964, pp. 22–23.

United States Commission on Civil Rights. *Jobs and Civil Rights: The Role of the Federal Government in Promoting Equal Opportunity in Employment and Training*. Prepared for the Commission by the Brookings Institution. Washington, D.C.: Brookings, 1969.

U.S. News & World Report. "The Equal Pay Law: How It Will Work." June 24, 1963, p. 10.

_____. "More Women in Top Government Jobs." March 16, 1964, p. 19.

Warner, David C., ed. *Toward New Human Rights: The Social Policies of the Kennedy and Johnson Administrations*. Austin, Texas: Lyndon B. Johnson School of Public Affairs, 1977.

Weeks, Christopher. *Job Corps: Dollars and Dropouts*. Boston: Little, Brown & Co., 1967.

Wicker, Tom. *JFK and LBJ: The Influence of Personality Upon Politics*. Baltimore: Penguin Books, 1969.

Index